*The
Bookselling
Business*

The Bookselling Business

Thomas Joy FRSA

Managing Director, Hatchards Ltd, Piccadilly, London
Past President, The Booksellers Association of Great Britain and Ireland
Past Chairman, Education Board, The Booksellers Association

Pitman Publishing

First published 1974

SIR ISAAC PITMAN AND SONS LTD.
Pitman House, Parker Street, Kingsway, London WC2B 5PB
P.O. Box 46038, Banda Street, Nairobi, Kenya

SIR ISAAC PITMAN (AUST.) PTY. LTD.
Pitman House, 158 Bouverie Street, Carlton, Victoria 3053, Australia

PITMAN PUBLISHING CORPORATION
6 East 43rd Street, New York, N.Y. 10017, U.S.A.

SIR ISAAC PITMAN (CANADA) LTD.
495 Wellington Street West, Toronto 135, Canada

THE COPP CLARK PUBLISHING COMPANY
517 Wellington Street West, Toronto 135, Canada

Printed in Great Britain by
Alden & Mowbray Ltd
at the Alden Press, Oxford

G1:16

Preface

This book endeavours to present a lucid and concise account of the business of bookselling today. It is, first, a *textbook* for book-shop managers, buyers and staff, and a guide to those starting new book businesses. It is also a reference book for publishers, librarians, reviewers, authors and all those who work in the book world. It includes those vital documents and facts to which people working with books must frequently refer and which are otherwise only available in leaflet or pamphlet form, and in practice usually difficult to find when required.

Based on my two earlier works—*Bookselling* published in 1952 and *The Truth about Bookselling* published in 1964, both out of print—*The Bookselling Business* is more than a revised edition of either of these: it is more comprehensive in scope and in the light of several years' further practical experience my general approach has often changed.

Acknowledgements

No one can write and compile a book of this nature without the enthusiastic support of the two trade organizations, the Booksellers Association of Great Britain and Ireland and the Publishers Association, and I acknowledge with gratitude their help and permission to reproduce documents and to quote from their publications. In particular I have used much valuable material from *Book Distribution: A Handbook for Booksellers and Publishers on the ordering and distribution of books in the United Kingdom.*

I am specially grateful to Mr R. E. Barker, Secretary of the Publishers Association, Mr G. R. Davies, Director of the Booksellers Association of Great Britain and Ireland, Mr Rupert Gowing, former Training Officer of the Booksellers Association, Mr W. A. Barnes, Secretary of Book Tokens Ltd, Mr Ben Winter-Goodwin, Managing Director of Book Centre Ltd, and Mr Martyn Goff, Director of the National Book League, who gave all the information required to present their services up to date.

I am grateful to Mr David Whitaker for permission to use material from *The Bookseller* and for the complete details of the Whitaker Reference Books.

I express my sincere appreciation to Mr Eric Bailey, Managing Director of University Bookshops (Oxford) Ltd (UBO), and to Mr Ian Miller, Training and Personnel Manager of Hudsons, Birmingham, for reading the greater part of the typescript and making important suggestions; and to Mr A. J. Bassett for help in detailing the computer system.

Above all, I thank Miss Mabel Riley, for typing this and all my books, for undertaking research, and for compiling the Index.

In acknowledging the above I must make it clear that the opinions expressed are my own and do not necessarily agree with the policies of either of the two trade associations or with the opinions of anyone who assisted me.

Thomas Joy

❈❈❈❈❈❈❈❈❈❈❈❈❈❈❈❈❈❈❈❈❈❈❈❈❈❈❈❈❈❈❈❈❈❈

Dedicated with affection
to
Sir William and Lady Collins
and to
Eric Bailey
President of The
Booksellers Association 1970–1972
and his wife Lauraine

Contents

✥✥✥✥✥✥✥✥✥✥✥✥✥✥✥✥✥✥✥✥✥✥✥✥✥✥✥✥✥✥✥✥✥✥✥✥✥

1

Introductory

Something over fifty years in bookselling now seems to me to be too short a period to justify claiming competence to write a textbook on the subject. One is continually learning and as years pass it becomes increasingly clear that although much of the practice of bookselling that I was originally taught in a bookshop at Oxford is still of value, a large amount is out of date. It is necessary for a bookseller to be abreast of the times not only with his buying of stock, but with the systems of successful retailing. He must get rid of old-fashioned methods which inhibit his business, but hold fast to that which is good in the old methods.

I believe a main reason for the demise of bookshops over the years, especially in the sixties, was largely their failure to move with the times, in particular as regards business methods. Many booksellers still indulge in too much unproductive work and continue to find reasons to avoid control of buying and expenses. Above all, some old-established booksellers fail to appreciate that with the loss of the 'carriage trade' people must be attracted into bookshops by improved window and interior displays.

Bookselling is a paradox, for, in looking back, many of the problems seem much the same today as when I entered the trade. For instance, booksellers are still 'fighting' for better terms, and many feel now, as then, that if they obtained increased discounts from the publishers, their problems would be over. In these days, however, overheads continue to increase rapidly and, although better terms would help, they are not likely in themselves to be sufficient to meet all the needs. Ever-increasing turnover is more essential than better terms; but above all it is vital to budget and to keep to that budget, thus ensuring every economy, particularly as regards the number of staff employed, and that the total expenditure on stock keeps within the budgeted figure. But 'Terms' are still a thorny subject and one of the controversies which, like others, remain with the trade decade after decade.

The paradox lies in the fact that although things seem to be so much the same there have, in fact, been almost imperceptible but very substantial changes over the years which, in writing this book, had to be recorded and analysed. One such change is 'Charter Membership', and I devote a chapter to it.

There are significant changes, too, in business methods and in training but perhaps the greatest change of all over the last fifty years is in the publishers' approach to 'Terms of Supply', which have changed slowly over the years, so slowly, in fact, that their true importance can be easily overlooked. Publishers have become marketing conscious and now co-operate in a variety of ways they did not do previously. Today they will often assist booksellers with their overstocks and with extra copies for display as well as with display stands, other display material and even at times with shelving. All these plus better discounts are having a marked effect; as a result many bookshops are improved and managers and staff better paid.

I wrote in *The Truth about Bookselling* that 'Bookselling is different' and although this has become a cliché it is a fact, and is the reason why most people in the trade differ from others in their approach to their job. Bookselling is more than a trade— it is a vocation. Few booksellers regard their shops simply as money-making enterprises: they believe good bookshops are at least as much a cultural necessity as the public libraries. All dedicated booksellers aim at catering for the cultural levels which exist, although they must vary according to locality, and many would rather shut up shop than sell trashy literature. It would surprise the public to know how careful most general booksellers are to exercise good taste and avoid displaying books which might prove offensive to their customers, so much so that even the covers of paperbacks are scrutinized to ensure acceptable standards of decency. Illustrations on covers of paperbacks or in the body of a work which, in the opinion of a book-buyer, are objectionable are likely to reduce drastically an order or to rule it out altogether. Yet the bookseller is not, and must not be, a censor.

Customers will complain from time to time that a book is indecent or offensive and here the bookseller must use his judgement, whether he agrees or not, and decide to stock or not to stock the book in question. He is expected, however, to obtain any book to meet an individual order and under the Charter Scheme has contracted so to do.

If a bookseller refuses to stock or to order a book because it might possibly offend customers he can hardly be said to be doing his job. Political books, religious books, biographies, art books, to say nothing of the modern novel and many classics of literature, can bring down on the poor bookseller's head the wrath of an ignorant, biased or bigoted customer. Throughout the ages writers and purveyors of books have been persecuted and there are always those who would censor books without full appreciation of the consequences to mankind. There is all too much ignorant talk and writing on this subject, but our very freedom is at stake. The more simple-minded see the problem as the banning of a particularly objectionable book on sex or sadism but the step is short, as history has proved, to suppression of books on religion, political thought and free-thinking generally. So, if freedom of expression is sometimes abused, it is better than Censorship. No individual or body, however well meaning or tolerant, can in the long term act as censor without causing grave injustices. '*Anyone who believes that there is some mystical sort of central fount of wisdom and right-thinking has already passed the point of no return on the sickeningly short journey from the rational man to the laboratory-conditioned mouse*', wrote Maurice Wiggin in *The Sunday Times*.

Maurice Wiggin here summed up brilliantly the opinion of most publishers and booksellers about freedom of expression. In the article from which I quote he was writing about television programmes, but the same is true of the printed word.

Good bookselling is an art and one which cannot be quickly acquired. It can be mastered only by years of practical experience. Almost daily applications are received from well-educated young men and women who wish to come into bookselling, believing it to be a nice, pleasant way of earning a living. I would be the last to discourage them, for so I have found it, but the way was, and still is, hard and success will usually only come after many years' experience.

In these days most booksellers are fully aware of the necessity for good shelving and fixtures, good lighting and attractive displays; but there is much more to successful trading than this. Most important of all, a bookshop attracts regular customers by the careful selection of stock and by the service to the customer.

Service must include, as I have already stated, the ordering of any book or pamphlet not in stock to meet a customer's needs. Such service can only be given by booksellers with complete and up-to-date reference books, the most important of which are detailed in Chapter 13; but even these cannot supplant the value of experience. The well-trained bookshop assistant should be a mine of information.

One of the most useful ways of gaining experience, other than in the bookshop itself, is to attend meetings of the Booksellers Association, since here one meets colleagues in the trade who are ever ready to talk over trade matters. Of course, publishers and their representatives are also most useful sources of information. Every bookseller will admit he owes much not only to both the Booksellers Association and the Publishers Association but also to publishers and their representatives.

There are courses of instruction arranged by the Training Committee of the Booksellers Association. Every assistant who wishes to become proficient and make rapid progress should study for a Diploma—not only because the Diploma is the accepted qualification in the trade—but because from the very first class attended or the first correspondence lesson studied the student is better informed and able to give a better service to customers.

Bookselling is a satisfying, worthwhile job of outstanding

interest and value and every bookseller I know is proud to be in 'The Trade'—few would change it for any other. 'Bookselling is a disease, once in the blood you can never lose it', I wrote in my autobiography *Mostly Joy*. This is true, so much so that booksellers find the trade all-absorbing and tend to be everlastingly talking shop. Most booksellers believe, rightly or wrongly, that they would have made much more money if they had gone into some other business. Doubtless many would, but they would have missed much.

Bookselling is truly a difficult and complex business and to run a business at a profit by the selling of new books only was, until recent years, an almost impossible feat. The coming of paperbacks has brought about considerable change and with their help many bookshops can prosper today without the addition of side-lines such as stationery and fancy goods, which were vitally necessary in the past to make the businesses pay.

In fact, the situation has so changed, owing to the ever-increasing sales of paperbacks, that in many bookshops they are an important and sometimes the larger part of turnover.

The terms of supply, to which I referred earlier, have changed for the better. When I first came into bookselling almost every book had to be ordered 'firm' and paid for. It was unusual to be allowed to return a book for credit if unsold. Very few publishers would, in those days, allow a bookseller to have stock 'on sale or return', even for special displays. Today publishers will often make a special arrangement for the return or exchange of at least a percentage of unsold stock, if the bookseller makes a special effort to sell his books. Nevertheless, bookselling is no quick road to fortune; most books must still be purchased 'firm' and, with well over 35,000 new titles published in Great Britain each year, the selection of books for stock constitutes a real problem. There is no doubt that booksellers are more prosperous than in past years and bookselling as a career offers better opportunities than ever before, but costs continue to rise and the benefit of increased turnover, which, in itself, is often largely the result of increase in price rather than increase in the number of books sold, is largely offset by the increase in wages, rents, rates, carriage charges, lighting, stationery and so on, so the position must be closely watched.

A good general bookseller is expected to have on his shelves the Standard Works, Dictionaries, Grammars and many classics of English Literature, as well as the best books in a wide field of General Literature, History, Travel, Biography, Psychology, Religion, Belles-Lettres, Children's Books and many more classifications. It is obviously impossible for him to have everything but, if customers repeatedly ask for titles and are disappointed at not seeing them in the shop, they will soon go elsewhere. The enormous number of new titles and the increased number of reprints make it impossible for even large shops to stock anything other than a small representative selection and, as I have said, the choice is no easy matter. If we assume that half the new publications each year are so specialized that the ordinary general bookseller need not stock them, we are left with an enormous number of new titles and there are many thousands of other British books in print, certainly over a quarter of a million.[1]

Every bookseller must endeavour to maintain a basic stock of books which will constantly sell and also represent new publications according to the anticipated demand.

The quantity of books purchased must naturally depend on the shelving, display space, capital available and the total sales expected in a normal trading year. This latter is important and will be dealt with more fully later. Booksellers, like any retailer, will fail if sufficient care is not taken to ensure that purchases and expenses bear a proper relation to turnover.

Another reason for failure, but one which is rarer today, is too much bad stock, so the 'marking down' or the 'writing off' of unsaleable or soiled stock must be given proper attention and dealt with systematically. Various systems in use in large and small businesses are described on pages 101–2. However skilled and experienced a book-buyer may be, he is bound to accumulate some books which will not sell. They may be good books but if they are not sold they gradually become out of date. Booksellers often find that where they have bought six copies of a

[1] *British Books in Print*, 1971, listed 240,000 titles from 5,600 publishers.

book, they have sold four; where they have bought three copies, they have sold two. In effect this means no profit at all. This problem, although not as serious, still exists in spite of improved conditions of supply, as all books cannot *automatically* be returned to the publishers for credit if unsold. Many members of the public think that unsold books can be returned to the publishers but such is not generally the case. The bookseller must buy and pay for his stock and anything left on his shelves for too long is ultimately dead stock. The odd unsold copy of a particular title is the main problem as publishers can rarely accept their return and it is all too easy for a bookseller to accumulate bad stock represented by hundreds of single copies of unsaleable books.

In practice, when a general book does not sell well in one bookshop it is usually 'slow' everywhere and both the bookseller and the publishers are eventually left with copies no one wants.

The National Book Sale has over the years helped in considerable measure to solve the over-stock problem and its working is explained in Chapter 19.

The reader will realize, then, that a successful bookseller must be a good book-buyer and a good businessman generally. There is obviously not the same risk in buying many other categories of merchandise as there is in the case of books, because most other stock—for instance, fancy goods and tobacco, or wearing apparel —will ultimately sell, although some reduction in price in the case of wearing apparel may be required. But with books, price reductions have to be pretty drastic to clear stocks effectively, which means selling off at a loss. With many other goods losses can more easily be borne, because of a larger margin of profit on sales or a quicker rate of turnover.

Overhead expenses are usually heavy in bookselling; the premises tend to be large to hold a good stock and a large, skilled staff is required to provide a good book service. The 'special order' service which is expected of every good bookseller is expensive to run and eats into profits.

Booksellers were perhaps the first traders to see the wisdom of self-service and to allow the public to browse around the shelves. In the USA many bookshops and book departments in departmental stores are now working on a self-service basis with 'check-out points', whereas booksellers in this country are reluctant to adopt completely self-service methods, deeming them to be contrary to the best standards of bookselling. The modern economics of retail trading are tending to force booksellers towards some combination of customer service and more self-service. Check-out points, particularly in paperback bookshops, are increasingly common in Great Britain as well as overseas. Actually, contrary to popular belief, there is little saving in labour costs in self-service bookshops if a moderately good service is to be provided, but one must admit that increased sales may result particularly if there is more face display of titles.

In bookselling the percentage of wages in relation to turnover tends to be high, so it pays to employ the best assistants available, to have the minimum number and to pay them well. An assistant who knows the job and is keen and energetic is worth two or three inexperienced ones, but even so there is a limit to what one man or woman can accomplish in a day.

In large measure bookselling is something of a seasonal business. Perhaps well over half the year's sales of books may be achieved in the Christmas shopping period, except in University towns. If over half the year's trade is done between October and December it brings with it certain problems and obviously staffing is one of them. In most shops extra staff is brought in to help with the Christmas rush but in bookselling the field of usefulness of temporary assistants is limited and there is practically no 'float' of experienced personnel. Consequently, a bookseller with a reputation for good service will have to maintain sufficient experienced staff throughout the year to be ready to deal with the trade at its peak periods, and it follows that he will to some extent be overstaffed for at least part of the year, and almost certainly running at a loss for some months. Some reserve of staff is usually vitally necessary during the summer holiday periods or in case of illness. Extra staff, even with previous bookselling experience, have to 'learn the stock' before they can be trusted to serve properly or look out mail orders. The trade knowledge and experience required in bookshops is far greater in extent than appears necessary to those outside the trade and it would surprise the general public to learn that every bookseller feels a little 'at sea' with his stock even after a short holiday break.

To sum up, a bookseller must have a sound knowledge of retailing methods which are common to the successful running of any kind of shop, but he must have more; he must have a flair for selecting the books his customers will buy, he must provide an efficient 'special order' service, and only consistent hard work and maximum efficiency will result in success.

I conclude that a first-class businessman can succeed in bookselling but that a love and appreciation of books alone is insufficient for success. I firmly believe also that the prospects for the trade and for the right people working in it have never been brighter.

2

The Economics of Bookselling

Some bookshops are lively, profitable businesses; others struggle to keep going. There is little doubt that, in spite of the great increase in sales, largely brought about by paperbacks, it is still a fact that most booksellers, *selling new books only*, without side-lines of stationery, fancy goods or second-hand books find it hard to pay rent, rates, staff and other usual overheads and to make a profit sufficient to give a good return on the capital involved. One cannot generalize on the difference between success and failure unless one sums it up in one word, MANAGEMENT. But Management means so many things, not only a clear under-standing of the economics of the trade, a lot of know-how and experience, but personality, drive, industry, enterprise, interest, vitality, humanity and flair. All one can do is to examine and comment on facts and figures.

Fortunately today booksellers have access to figures which give an accurate picture of average expenses and profits in book-selling and although overall the picture is not a particularly bright one there is plenty of scope for existing booksellers and for new bookshops.

The figures to which I refer are compiled annually and are detailed in The Economic Survey of the Charter Group of the Booksellers Association of Great Britain and Ireland.[1] These annual 'Results of Bookselling' are based on figures obtained from members of the Charter Group, so from the results of around 250 firms, varying in size, statistics are provided giving

[1] Charter Bookselling is described in Chapter 16.

average profits in various categories of bookshops with a break-down of expenses, etc.

Of course, there are no simple answers to the many problems besetting booksellers, since much depends on the varying factors. Bookseller *A* has a long lease and a good site, with a cheap rent; Bookseller *B* is not so fortunate, but his shop is near schools or in a university town, which gives him a larger number of book-buying residents, so, although his rent is higher than that of Bookseller *A*, the extra volume of trade enables him to afford a higher rent. No two are the same.

It is obvious that geographical position, the size of local population and the kind of population will affect a bookseller's trade and turnover and, however keen a businessman the bookseller may be, the possibilities of his business are usually limited to some extent by his geographical position and premises.

A look at gross-profit margins alone can be misleading. Nevertheless it is reasonable to ask what gross profit can a book-seller expect? The majority of books ordered before publication or for stock replacement, other than school textbooks, scientific, technical and medical books and a large range of specialized publications, are sold to the bookseller by the publisher at a third off published price or at best 35 per cent off, rarely more; that is to say, a book which sells at 75p usually costs the book-seller 50p, but by buying a quantity of a title or by having a large account with a publisher he may get better terms, particularly for paperbacks. However, not only the exceptions mentioned above but also single copies ordered to meet special requirements of customers or for stock, frequently do not enjoy these terms, and even where they do, the costs of ordering and postage reduce the profit considerably and many such transactions result in a financial loss to the bookseller. It could be said that the better the service the bookseller renders the greater the difficulty of making a profit. Of course, bad stock or losses by theft also reduce gross profit.

If a bookseller supplies schools he will be expected to give a discount off purchases of school textbooks, most being non-net, and terms on school textbooks are lower (usually 16⅔ to 21 per

cent) than on *net* books. If he supplies public or county libraries
they will almost certainly have a licence which enables the bookseller, if named thereon, to give a discount of 10 per cent on net
books. It is obvious that with these variations in trade terms and
discounts no gross-profit figure can be given to cover all bookshops, but somewhere between 22 and 30 per cent, with an
average around 27 or 28 per cent, is about as near as one can get
for general bookselling. A bookseller selling mostly new, general
books, which he obtains from the publisher at a discount of 33⅓
per cent (i.e. one-third off published price) or more, may expect
a gross-profit figure of between 27 and 30 per cent, and if it is
much lower it is likely that he is either having stock stolen or
money taken from the till or he has been obliged to sell off at
reduced prices a considerable quantity of bad stock. A bookseller whose business is very largely that of supplying schools or
libraries may well have a gross-profit figure as low as 22 per cent
or even less, yet it may well be a more profitable business than
that of a general bookseller with a gross-profit of, say, 28 per cent.
It is necessary to understand that, whatever the gross-profit
figure, the success of a business depends on the volume of trade,
rate of stock-turn, and reasonable overheads. The more books
sold the greater the profit, if a shop is properly run. Some of the
most successful booksellers are those who *go out* for trade by
contacting headmasters, librarians and secretaries of institutions
personally wherever possible, or through the post, rather than
sitting in the shop waiting for customers to call in. But some
booksellers, greedy for turnover, or believing that the goodwill
will bring extra business, take on school or library business at
terms and with services which are uneconomic, and this can be a
mistake. No one can succeed working at a loss yet all too often I
have seen booksellers facing financial difficulties because they
gave too big discounts to schools or supplied large quantities of
books to slow-paying bodies.

A member of the shopping public might consider a bookseller's
margin of profit of 50p on a £1.50 publication to be high.
'What', he might ask, 'does he do to deserve it?' In the first place,
examination of the accounts of any bookseller in Great Britain

will satisfy an accountant that a bookseller's net profit is indeed small, and that better terms are required for a healthy trade. Secondly, although it cannot be denied that from time to time a bookseller is fortunate when there is a quick-selling book at a good price and profit, such is not the complete picture and conclusions can be drawn only when one has the matter in perspective. Generally, the bookseller will stock thousands of books which sell slowly overall, and some not at all. It must be remembered that *bookshops are the publishers' showrooms.* They do more than meet demand, they create it, and thus are vital to the cultural welfare of the community. Such *showrooms* are expensive to run, they need space, and rents are costly, so much so that few bookshops can afford to have premises in the High Street. They need good lighting, well-constructed fixtures and, above all, skilled staff, and all these cost money. Remember, too, that there are a thousand and one incidentals, from paper and string to telephones and typewriters, all of which have to be paid for out of the discounts which publishers allow booksellers.

But surely, it could be argued, these expenses apply to most forms of retailing and, of course, they do. But as I have already stressed, books are different. A bookseller is expected to order any book required and this service is costly in time, postage, stationery and telephone calls, and involves the handling of thousands of small invoices and accounts for small amounts from up to 2,000 publishers. The public would be surprised to know that such service, usually provided free, is run generally at a considerable loss. Another problem is *bad stock.* Even when unsold copies can be returned to the publisher, postage, packing and labour are costly. All too frequently a book which does not sell at the full published price can only be sold, if at all, at a considerable loss. Too slow a turnover is another real problem with many booksellers and a reason why so many have a struggle to keep in business and why very few make large profits.

To sell more books is the *key* to success and the delight of possession, as distinct from the reading of books, is fortunately becoming increasingly instilled into the minds of a large percentage of the British public.

As a result of a more affluent society, better cultural opportunities and television and radio programmes there is an ever-
increasing demand for reading in ever-widening classifications, as
witness the success of the paperback and the substantial annual
increase in public-library issues. In the past we have been a nation
of book *borrowers* rather than of book *buyers* but today I see the
beginning of a great change. At last more people want to possess
books, not just to read them. In the same way as they do not want
merely to hear a gramophone record once, but to possess it, to
be able to play it again, so they want books on their shelves to
enjoy again and again.

Most of Britain's great commercial libraries are now gone,
largely as a result of the increase in the quantity of light reading
matter issued free by our public and county libraries and as a
result of social change—it is no longer *infra dig.* to borrow from
a free library. Doubtless, too, paperbacks had a considerable
influence. Public libraries have not only put commercial libraries
out of business but in some ways have adversely affected bookselling. Fiction sales, for instance, would be increased if libraries
did not supply popular reading free. One must not forget,
however, that all libraries help form and cultivate the reading
habit, and there would be little future in bookselling without
them, but from a bookseller's angle it would be better if public
libraries were more in the nature of reference libraries and did not
compete by circulating to such a large degree the latest light
reading matter. Yet the regular buying by public libraries of
books from local bookshops keeps many booksellers in business;
their buying helps in keeping down the price of books and it is
argued that many books would not be published but for the
library demand. So if public libraries are a mixed blessing they are
still of vital importance to successful bookselling and publishing.

A general bookseller must endeavour to keep his stock down to
a figure which will result in a stock-turn of at least three to four
times a year. Some would say four to five times is the figure.
Some university and specialized booksellers, particularly those
with second-hand book departments, can have a slower turnover
and still make a profit, but usually turnover must be at least three

or four times a year for a healthy book business, and I think five is a figure at which to aim in general bookselling. The tendency is for booksellers to have too much stock and to keep too much too long. Books which do not sell well are a drag on the business, and booksellers must, in these days, be more ready to work with smaller stocks and to take full advantage of the National Book Sales to clear out old stock.

A few of the more venturesome booksellers are succeeding in increasing turnover and yet reducing stock. A few have reduced stock by a half or more, in spite of rising prices, and yet increased sales considerably. This is achieved by systems of more face display and better stock control to ensure that quick-selling titles are reordered in good time and in the right quantity. Book-buying in many shops will continue to rely on the bookseller's memory and skill but some stock-control system is often necessary.

Paperbacks sell rapidly so the replacement of stock without delay is tremendously important in this field. Most general booksellers these days represent paperbacks in a big way and their sale may constitute a considerable portion of the bookshop's turnover, but hardback sales continue to be the main business in the bookshops, so the hardback stock must be well displayed and so classified that the maximum sales are obtained. The dusty top shelves which no customer can reach are, or should be, things of the past.

In the 1950's to the 1960's a reduction in the number of good stock-holding bookshops caused publishers great concern because a number went out of business, and these were by no means all small, unimportant concerns. Once a bookshop closes much of the trade is lost, as every bookshop increases business in books simply by being there and every good book service encourages interest in books and stimulates sales. There are signs that the number of bookshops is now on the increase rather than the reverse. How far the situation is being improved by better trade terms is anyone's guess. Better terms, together with improved conditions of supply and a more affluent book-loving society are all contributing factors.

My earliest recollections in bookselling include the disputes and troubles over trade terms. It is likely that booksellers and publishers have argued over them for centuries but, as far as I can go back, booksellers have complained that the trade terms were not sufficiently good to enable them to stay in business. I recall publishers who would not give more than 25 per cent discount, and some Oxford booksellers in those days agreed not to display, but only obtain to order, books from publishers whose terms were considered to be far too low. Battles raged and there were diehard publishers who held the view that, if booksellers were given better terms than 25 per cent, they would want 30 per cent, then 33⅓ per cent and so on to 40 per cent or more, and it could be argued that history has proved them right. Many publishers, however, realized the importance of keeping their retail outlets (the bookshops) healthy, and were ready to improve trade terms from time to time to meet ever changing trading conditions. During recent years the business relationship between publishers and booksellers has improved beyond recognition, and for this great credit is due to the Officers and Council Members of the Booksellers and Publishers Associations who worked patiently over long years to bring about close and friendly relations, withstanding the efforts of the wilder characters in the trade who, from time to time, were forceful in advocating at branch meetings and conferences that action be taken to *make* publishers toe the line. Wiser counsels prevailed and patience, tact and increased trust have resulted in recent years in substantially improved discounts and in the better conditions of supply.

Still many booksellers, like Oliver Twist, 'ask for more', as they find it difficult to meet ever-increasing overheads. Of course, publishers, too, have this problem but the publishers fix the published prices of their books, which must cover their own overheads, and it is argued that they could also take into consideration the need of the bookseller to meet his overheads and price their books to enable them to give the best possible terms to booksellers. What is certain is that the prosperity of the trade as a whole relies on a network of financially healthy bookshops throughout the country. The Export trade in books is of great national importance, being *over one per cent* of the total

Exports of Great Britain. This is to no small extent due to a healthy home market, which helps in keeping prices competitive.

These are difficult times for shopkeepers, particularly small shopkeepers, and it will be increasingly difficult for them to remain in the main streets, with the enormous rents required. They are further handicapped by having to keep their shops open to serve the public on Saturdays and late evenings, so working hours in shops are not as attractive as in other industries. Wages of assistants, also, are still low down on the industrial scale, but over recent years there has been considerable improvement and opportunities for promotion are better than in the past.

It has long been considered desirable that every town should have at least one good bookshop, and obviously a good bookshop must be a well-run and prosperous business; but good booksellers are scarce.

To return to the vexed question of terms, it is obvious that better terms are needed by booksellers. Somewhere between 35 and 40 per cent is required, if the trade and all engaged in it are to prosper. When shops are staffed with fully-qualified, experienced, well-paid and *keen* personnel, the takings of each assistant are greater, more books are sold, printing orders are larger and published prices can be reduced. The prosperity of publishers obviously depends on the efficiency of the retail outlets, so both booksellers and publishers must continue to get down to the business of planning together to encourage and reward better bookselling. Sound trading margins are admittedly required, but there is more to it than that, as publishers are well aware, which is why they will often supply free displays stands and other sales aids and co-operate in a number of ways to the bookseller's advantage.

For many years I advocated extra discounts for booksellers who order quantities of a title and now these are often available. It was an extraordinary situation when a bookseller ordering some hundreds of a title could usually only get them at the same price as another ordering two or three or even a single copy. In retailing generally, better discounts are obtainable for quantity orders and a similar inducement is obviously necessary in bookselling. I wrote in 1964: 'At present publishers' representatives are more often than not met with sales resistance on the part of the book buyer. . . . How different the position might be for them were a book buyer to stand to gain by ordering the right quantity on subscription and were he to lose the chance of the best discounts by under-ordering.' The position has improved since 1964.

Quantity terms, it can be argued, can be of help only to the large booksellers, and the majority, being small businesses, could not order in large quantities, whatever the terms. The aim of the booksellers has been to try to obtain a discount of at least 33⅓ per cent even on single-copy orders, but at these terms there is still a large percentage of uneconomic bookselling. Although much progress has been made in the direction of better terms there is a long way to go before booksellers, particularly small ones, get a true *overall* 'third off'. Some publishers give lower discounts on single-copy orders and hope the better terms of 33⅓ per cent on orders for two or three copies or more will induce booksellers to buy more than one copy. The important thing is for publishers to adjust terms to permit quality booksellers, *however small*, to survive. The allocation of extra discounts for quantity orders seems to me to be reasonable and businesslike, but one should remember that *success* in bookselling lies in modest orders, repeated as soon as stocks are low or sold out, rather than in orders for quantities of a title which are so large that it will take months or years to sell out; secondly success lies in concentration on salesmanship and the sales-promotion side of the business; and, finally, in careful 'control' of every book purchased, so that old stock does not accumulate. 'There is no doubt the more progressive members of the trade seem to be able to achieve a rate of stock turnover considerably greater than that of less successful businesses.' This quotation is from a publication, *Results of Bookselling, 1948–1952*, and it is even more true today.

I have one or two 'rules of thumb' which over the years have served me in good stead. The first is that salaries and wages together should never total more than half the gross-profit percentage and, if possible, rather less. The *Economic Surveys* over the years supports this. For instance, where the gross profit is, say, 26 per cent, total wages, salaries, NHI, and any expense connected with wages such as Luncheon Vouchers, should not exceed 13 per cent of the gross-profit figure as a percentage of sales. Secondly, if the gross-profit figure is much too low or suddenly drops, I would suspect the theft of books or cash, or a combination of both. There could be other reasons but in my experience a sudden drop is likely to be due to dishonesty. Thirdly, as I said earlier, a stock-turn in general bookselling of between four to five times is to be aimed at. Where the stock-turn is much lower the stock is likely to be too high. Reduce it! Lastly, it is costly in tax to take stock at too high a figure. I shall deal with this in the chapter on Stocktaking (Chapter 12).

3

The Net Book Agreement

'Books are different', which is why they are zero-rated for Value Added Tax (see page 194). British books were previously exempt from purchase tax and, above all, they are an exception to the laws against price maintenance as Net Books must be sold to the public only at the *full published price*.

The Net Book Agreement is the most important governing factor in British bookselling and publishing and it is vital that every bookseller thoroughly understands it and knows something of its history, for every bookseller dealing in new books *must* abide by the terms of the Net Book Agreement, 1957, and should he fail to do so he may be penalized.

This 1957 Agreement is the one which made history when it was upheld by the Restrictive Practices Court in October 1962. The Restrictive Practices Court, in a reserved judgement, declared that '*the restrictions in the Net Book Agreement were NOT contrary to the public interest*'. The Court found that 'the abrogation of the Agreement would result in fewer and less well-equipped stock-holding bookshops, more expensive books and fewer published titles'. The Court held that 'the avoidance of ANY ONE of these consequences would be sufficient justification for the continuance of the Agreement'.

Further on in this chapter a little is given of the history of this and previous Net Book Agreements, with quotations from the judgement and other authoritative sources proving that the Agreement is in the interests of the public as well as of every bookseller and publisher. Needless to say, it must be strictly adhered to, as the Agreement, upheld by the Restrictive Practices Court, is enforceable.

To get the Net Book Agreement clearly in mind I suggest it is best to start by accepting simply that a *new net book must always be sold at the full published price*. It does not matter how large the order, how good the customer, or how worthy the charity; no discount can be given on net books. Such considerations have no bearing on the basic fact that 'net' means 'net'. Once that is understood, we can make the qualification that certain public libraries can be given a discount of 10 per cent, but only if the bookseller has his name registered on the library licence for the particular library to which he is giving discount.

The full Net Book Agreement is included at the end of this chapter and must be studied with care, but if the above brief summary is clearly understood the rest of the Agreement will present no difficulties. Should a bookseller fail to abide by the Net Book Agreement of 1957 he could find himself in serious trouble. He could be taken to court by the Publishers Association on behalf of the contracting signatories and an action at law could be costly as well as damaging to a bookseller's reputation.

It is necessary for me to qualify my generalization that net books must always be sold at the full published price by drawing attention to the clauses in the Agreement regarding books which a bookseller has had in stock for over twelve months (Net Book Agreement, Clause ii); also to the rarely used but important Quantity Book Buying Scheme (see page 180).

But what is a 'net' book? Almost all books handled by the bookseller, including scientific, technical and medical books, are 'net' books. The word 'net' is usually printed after the price on the dust-jacket, and many publishers use it or some abbreviation (such as 'N') on their invoices. Publishers' invoices usually have a clause printed at the foot as follows: 'Net books are supplied subject to the Publishers Association standard condition of sale registered under the Restrictive Trade Practice Act 1956', or more simply: 'Net Books must not be sold to the public at less than the published price'.

As I have said, the simplest way to comprehend the Net Book

Agreement is to accept that all net books must be sold at the *full published price*. On no account can discount be given, or *consideration of any kind*. It is a breach of the Agreement to try to avoid its terms by paying travelling expenses or by giving an extra copy free of a book or other goods. No discount can be given for books intended for a charitable purpose, for a school or college, or for a library. The only exception is in the case of public and county libraries, and when such libraries have *library licences* they can be given a discount of up to 10 per cent, but only by the bookseller named by the library and appearing on the licence as being a supplier.

It must be emphasized this does not mean that *any* bookseller can give *any* county or public library the discount of up to 10 per cent. Before the discount can be granted, the bookseller must be licensed to give the discount to the particular library. When this has been done, the bookseller receives his copy of the licence and then, and only then, is he entitled to give a discount. These licences are issued solely by the authority of the Publishers Association as the duly authorized agent of all publishers signatory to the Net Book Agreement, as indeed are any other authorizations permitting an exception to the absolute maintenance of net book prices.

Before obtaining books at trade terms *from publishers*, booksellers are asked to acknowledge in writing that they have been notified of the Standard Conditions of Sale of Net Books as set out in the Net Book Agreement. Booksellers obtaining stocks through wholesalers must similarly observe the terms of the Net Book Agreement and should know the conditions under which their stock is supplied.

Any second-hand net book in new or soiled condition bought by the bookseller from, say, a reviewer, may not be sold at less than the full published price within six months of publication, and not only may it not be sold but it is a breach of the Agreement *to offer it for sale* at less than the full published price before the six months' period has elapsed.

No stock of net books can be treated as unsaleable or bad stock and sold at less than the full published price within twelve months of the date of the latest purchase of any copy, and even then such stock must first be offered back to the publisher at cost price or at the proposed reduced price, whichever is the lower. The Net Book Agreement applies also to sales for export.

Non-Net Books

Non-net or 'subject' books are, in the main, school textbooks. Some Children's 'Rewards', too, are included. Non-net books have a published price but a discount can be given to anyone at the discretion of the bookseller; normally, however, a discount is only given to Educational Authorities. The discount may vary from 5 per cent to as much as 12½ per cent. Even higher discounts have been offered, but they seldom prove viable. Discounts are not usually given to customers on individual books sold in the bookshop. In fact many booksellers have to price individual non-net books for sale off their shelves at slightly higher prices than the publishers' catalogue prices, which are designed for sales in quantity to Educational Authorities, simply to cover their over-heads on such sales. As the publishers' discounts on these non-net educational books are lower than those usually given on net books, it follows that the bookseller is passing on part of his possible profit by allowing discount. Firms dealing in educational books in a large way in most cases also sell quantities of other goods which carry larger trading margins, including *net* books which must, of course, be sold at the full published price. School-prizes Accounts, for instance, are of value to a bookseller, as many books are likely to be net, and educational booksellers often benefit from the sale of stationery and other school equipment.

The Net Book Agreement should be studied carefully from time to time by everyone engaged in bookselling, and the following notes will be helpful particularly to those who know little of its history.

The Net Book System
Reasons for its Introduction

In the latter half of the nineteenth century the trade in new books was so seriously affected by the *uncontrolled competition in discounts* given to the public from the published price of books that it could not be carried on at a profit and often entailed loss, the financial return being insufficient to cover working expenses. As a result the number of booksellers keeping stocks of high-class new books steadily diminished, and men of ability, who otherwise would have followed the family tradition and indulged a love of literature by becoming booksellers, were diverted to other lines of business. This result was detrimental not only to authors, publishers and booksellers but also to the general public, including schools, libraries and institutions, who could not find adequate facilities for seeing and purchasing books. Proof of this state of affairs may be found in the following quotations.

Report of the Society of Authors, 1897

'Your Committee desire at the outset to endorse the statements as to the present depressed state of the retail trade. Injury to the Bookseller must partly fall upon the author, since much of his own welfare must be bound up with the prosperity of the Book-seller. Many books, indeed, cannot be said to be effectively published until the Booksellers are interested in them; and no Bookseller can be said to be interested in a book unless he gains a fair profit from selling it. In the general interest of literature, moreover, it is important that the race of trained and intelligent Booksellers in the country should not be crowded out of existence.'

Publishers Association Meeting, 1897: Statement by leading publishers

'It is not stated that Booksellers as a whole do not make a profit, but that the profit is derived from the sale of non-copyright literature, stationery and fancy goods, while the margin on copyright books, with which the members of this Association are concerned, barely suffices to pay working expenses. . . . This state of things . . . is due solely to the pressure of competition which drives Booksellers to offer continually better and better terms to their customers, and forces Publishers to keep pace by allowing larger and larger discounts from the retail price to the trade.'

Introduction of the System

After prolonged discussions the Associated Booksellers of Great Britain and Ireland (founded in 1895) and the Publishers Association (founded in the following year) agreed that some form of control over the prices at which books were sold to the public was essential to the continuance of the book trade, and that this should take the form of issuing books at rather lower prices, which were for cash and *strictly net*, no discount being allowable to anybody other than a bookseller. This method has gradually extended to all classes of books, except some produced for and sold, mostly in bulk, to schools. It was thus referred to by a public librarian (*vide The Author*, 1904): 'The system is that it removes the competition from one of cutting to one of competency.'

Its Beneficial Results

It has enabled the sale of new books to be carried on without loss and with some modest profit, enough to attract once more into the book trade a well-educated type of man and woman, who with their staffs are trying to serve the community well and to make bookshops 'a centre of literary and artistic interest and enlightenment—a place where the best books, new and old, can be inspected at leisure' (*vide* 'The Report of Sir Henry Newbolt's Committee on the Teaching of English in England', HM Stationery Office, 1921).

Advantages to the Book-Buyer

If proof were needed that the intention of the net book system is not an attempt to maintain unduly high prices or excessive margins of profit, it may be found in the evidences and summing-up of the case presented in the Restrictive Practices Court.

The following extracts from the judgement of the Net Book Agreement—printed in full in *The Bookseller*, 3 November 1962—should suffice to convince any sceptic. (The headings are mine.)

WITHOUT THE AGREEMENT BOOKS WOULD COST MORE

'The evidence of publishers who believe prices would be higher if the Agreement came to an end rests largely, if not mainly, on calculations about the size of printing orders. In the absence of retail price maintenance, it is said, publishers would be reluctant to print as many copies at one time as they do now, and a reduction in the number printed would necessarily increase the cost of producing each copy. It must be true that a smaller printing order would make each separate copy more expensive.'

WITHOUT THE AGREEMENT THERE WOULD BE FEWER BOOKSHOPS, FEWER NEW TITLES

'The respondents have satisfied us that abrogation of the Net Book Agreement would produce the following results. The number of stockholding booksellers in the country would be reduced. The stocks held by the surviving stockholding booksellers would be less extensive and less varied than at present. Although in rare cases retail purchasers might be able to buy particular titles more cheaply than if the Agreement remained in force, the retail price of most books would be higher. Fewer titles would be published, and those which failed to find a publisher in consequence of the altered conditions resulting from the abrogation of the Agreement would include works of probable literary or scholastic value.'

WITHOUT THE AGREEMENT EVEN LIBRARIES WOULD HAVE TO PAY MORE

'We do not think that the net result of the abrogation of the Net Book Agreement would be advantageous for any public libraries and certainly not those of smaller library authorities; on the contrary, we think that generally they would have to pay more for their books than under present circumstances, although in some cases not so much more as an ordinary member of the public would have to pay.'

The Net Book Agreement, 1957, is set out in full on pages 27–8. A list of signatories to the agreement is obtainable on request from the Publishers Association.

THE PUBLISHERS ASSOCIATION

19 BEDFORD SQUARE, W.C.1

NET BOOK AGREEMENT, 1957

𝕎𝕖 the undersigned several firms of publishers, being desirous that in so far as we publish books at net prices (as to which each publisher is free to make his own decisions), those net prices shall normally be the prices at which such books are sold to the public as hereinafter defined, and in order to avoid disorganisation in the book trade and to ensure that the public may be informed of and able uniformly to take advantage of the conditions under which net books may be sold at less than the net prices, hereby agree to adopt and each of us does hereby adopt the following standard sale conditions for the net books published by us within the United Kingdom:

STANDARD CONDITIONS OF SALE OF NET BOOKS

(i) Except as provided in clauses (ii) to (iv) hereof and except as we may otherwise direct net books shall not be sold or offered for sale or caused or permitted to be sold or offered for sale to the public at less than the net published prices.

(ii) A net book may be sold or offered for sale to the public at less than the net published price if
(a) it has been held in stock by the bookseller for a period of more than twelve months from the date of the latest purchase by him of any copy thereof and
(b) it has been offered to the publisher at cost price or at the proposed reduced price whichever shall be the lower and such offer has been refused by the publisher.

(iii) A net book may be sold or offered for sale to the public at less than the published price if it is second-hand and six months have elapsed since its date of publication.

(iv) A net book may be sold at a discount to such libraries, book agents (including Service Unit libraries), quantity buyers and institutions as are from time to time authorised by the Council of The Publishers Associations of such amount and on such conditions as are laid down in the instrument of authorisation. Such amount and conditions shall not initially be less or less favourable than those prevailing at the date of this Agreement.

(v) For the purposes of clause (i) hereof a book shall be considered as sold at less than the net published price if the bookseller
(a) offers or gives any consideration in cash to any purchaser except under licence from the Council of The Publishers Association or

(*b*) offers or gives any consideration in kind (e.g. card indexing, stamping, reinforced bindings, etc., at less than the actual cost thereof to the bookseller).

(vi) For the purposes of this Agreement and of these Standard Conditions:
Net book shall mean a book, pamphlet, map or other similar printed matter published at a net price. *Net price* and *net published price* shall mean the price fixed from time to time by the publisher below which the net book shall not be sold to the public.
Public shall be deemed to include schools, libraries, institutions and other non-trading bodies.
Person shall include any company, firm, corporation, club, institution, organisation, association or other body.

(vii) The above conditions shall apply to all sales executed in the United Kingdom and the Republic of Ireland whether effected by wholesaler or retailer when the publisher's immediate trade customer, whether wholesaler or retailer, or the wholesaler's immediate trade customer, is in the United Kingdom or the Republic of Ireland.

We the undersigned several firms of publishers further agree to appoint and each of us does hereby appoint the Council of The Publishers Association to act as our agent in the collection of information concerning breaches of contract by persons selling or offering for sale net books, and in keeping each individual publisher informed of breaches in respect of such net books as are published by him and we further hereby undertake and agree that we will each enforce our contractual rights and our rights under the Restrictive Trade Practices Act 1956 if called upon to do so by the Council of The Publishers Association, and provided that we shall be indemnified by The Publishers Association if so requested by us in respect of any costs of such action incurred by us or by the Council of The Publishers Association on our behalf.

4

Buying

Many booksellers, particularly those of the old school, regard buying as being the most important function of booksellers, but in my experience buying can be delegated, whereas many functions of top management cannot. So I emphasize that selling, and by that I mean all those things linked with sales promotion, is of primary importance and buying must never intrude to the extent that it interferes with the expansion of the business. It was possible in past years for a bookseller to see all publishers' representatives and at the same time to manage the business, but there are many more publishers today and many more books published, so only in comparatively small businesses should all the buying as well as general management be undertaken by one person. In London the whole day and every day can be taken up by seeing publishers' representatives and buying the new books and reordering older titles. Unless this is delegated in part or in whole the business must suffer.

New books are customarily 'subscribed' by publishers' representatives. They pay regular visits, sometimes as often as once a week to large bookshops, less frequently in smaller towns and to small shops. The representative will usually first show the new publications and secondly inquire if there are any repeat orders for stock items. These days representatives frequently check their stock lists with assistants in charge of certain classifications on the shop floor before reporting to the chief buyer.

Though they vary in their approach and method, publishers' representatives are very valuable friends of booksellers, so the first thing a good bookseller should learn is to avoid keeping a representative waiting. He must be afforded the dignity of his position and treated with courtesy and respect. If it is not convenient to deal with him immediately, the bookseller should greet him and say when he will be able to see him, as it may be possible for the representative to make another call and to return at a more convenient time. Courtesy to publishers' representatives, as every bookseller knows, is fundamental in running a book business successfully. The representative can advise you when the publisher's stocks are running low, he can tell you how a book is selling, and in a variety of ways ensure that his bookseller customers are not losing business. Although all this may seem obvious, representatives do not always receive the courtesy they deserve.

Ordering Books

Having looked at the books and decided which he wishes to buy, and the number of copies, the bookseller must *write* an order, preferably using the Standard Order Form (see page 40). Some small bookshops give verbal orders, and note the details as the order is given; obviously this is an unbusinesslike procedure. Most bookshops have printed order books more or less falling in line with the Standard Order Form, with the firm's name and address and other relevant details. It is, of course, important that every order should have a number, and numbered order books are usually printed with two pages for each number, one being retained in the book as a carbon copy. Most booksellers, when ordering, write the title, the published price and number of copies required. In the case of general books the terms 'On Subscription' (i.e. ordered in advance of publication) or 'Traveller's Order' are usually $33\frac{1}{3}$ or 35 per cent—sometimes more for large quantities.

If any special arrangements are made with the representative regarding the date of delivery, date of invoice, or 'On Sale or Return' or 'See Safe' terms, they should be written on the order to prevent misunderstandings arising later.

Unless otherwise agreed beforehand, a bookseller's orders are treated as firm, which means that the bookseller will accept the books and pay for them, and he will not subsequently expect to return any of them without the prior agreement of the publisher. Exceptionally, with the concurrence of the publisher, a bookseller may order books 'On Sale or Return', 'See Safe', 'On Consignment', or 'On Approval'. The accepted definition of these terms are:

(a) *On Sale or Return* (normally for a specified period). I wrote in my previous books that 'On Sale' books are not usually charged by the publisher and *payment is not due until the end of the specified period or, if no time limit is laid down, payment is due when the books are sold*. With computerization, however, the situation has changed and books are usually charged, but payment is still not due until the books are sold or at the end of a specified period. In large measure 'See Safe' arrangements have taken the place of 'On Sale'. A bookseller still has the right to return all 'On Sale' stock *for credit* (i.e. to be offset against the charge that would otherwise be made) within the agreed period.

The best procedure for the bookseller is to keep the 'On Sale' invoices in a separate file until the stock is sold or that part which remains unsold is returned. The invoice is passed at the same time as the credit note or the bookseller may accept a revised invoice for the number of copies actually sold. It is advisable to record all 'On Sale' books in a special index in order that the stock may be assembled and returned at regular intervals or at the end of the specified period: otherwise there is a danger that some 'On Sale' books will be overlooked, bought and paid for, and treated as part of the bookseller's stock. It is also advisable to make some mark inside all books held 'On Sale or Return' (O/S is a common way of marking this stock), the value of the mark being that at stocktaking time these books can be identified and returned if they have been overlooked, assuming it is not too late. It is important that unsold stock supplied 'On Sale' should be returned promptly and in good condition. Outward carriage is subject to the publisher's normal rules, and the bookseller is responsible for return carriage unless other arrangements are made.

(b) *See Safe* (normally for a specified period). *The books are charged in the current account and the bookseller is liable for payment in full.* He has, however, the right to return any unsold copies for credit within an agreed period. Credit may be given or an order for other books to value to offset the credit may be expected, so whatever is agreed at the time of ordering it should be written on the order to avoid dispute at a later date. Carriage arrangements are the same as for 'On Sale or Return'.

(c) *On Consignment* (normally for a specified period). The books are either charged on a *pro forma* invoice, or dispatched with an advice note. They remain the publisher's property and are only charged as reported sold by the bookseller. Carriage arrangements are as for 'On Sale or Return'.

(d) *On Approval.* Publishers are usually willing to send a copy of a book on approval, if a bookseller wishes to show a copy to a special customer. The book is sometimes charged firm and credited if returned. Carriage arrangements are the same as those mentioned above.

'See Safe' is rather a loose term and a clear understanding of its meaning should, as I have said, be obtained in each case and noted. It is not unknown for a bookseller to have a large quantity of a book on a 'See Safe' basis, only to find (when the time comes to exchange the unsold stock) that the publisher's representative has left the firm and the trade manager of the publisher has no record that the stock was supplied 'See Safe'.

It is always grossly unfair for a bookseller to accept books 'On Sale or Return' or 'See Safe' unless he feels he has a good chance of selling them and will display them at least as well as the stock he has bought firm. Publishers have complained from time to time that booksellers do not display or try to sell books which have been supplied 'On Sale or Return', preferring to 'push' stock they have actually bought. Such an attitude on the part of the book-seller is understandable, but it would be fairer to the publisher not to accept any stock unless a real effort will be made to sell it, and this 'hiding' of stock by the bookseller has doubtless often influenced publishers to refuse to extend the practice of 'On Sale'.

On the other hand publishers must be reasonable as regards condition of returned stock. The bookseller who does his best by displaying and keeping books before the public in the hope of selling them will surely sell more, but the stock returned by him will not be as fresh as stock from a bookseller who left the stock in the original packets.

New books are usually ordered from the publisher's representa-tive, or in remote areas from advance publicity of one kind or another. It is necessary from time to time to reorder stock lines; country booksellers in particular look forward to the visits of publishers' representatives, as they secure best terms (journey terms) on travellers' orders.

The representatives, of course, provide valuable information regarding new books and will also inquire about other books on their lists which they remember the bookseller took originally and which they know are selling well. A bookseller who has been buying for a period of years will know most of the representatives and have a good idea of each one's judgement regarding the books which are most likely to sell. Experienced representatives can frequently say in advance how many copies will be ordered by each buyer, and they have a knowledge of the kind of book for which each bookseller has a market, so their advice must not be ignored.

There is a small handbook issued by the Book Publishers' Representatives Association which gives the names and addresses of most of the publishers' representatives, the firms they represent, and the territory covered by each individual. This is provided free of charge and is a helpful 'trade tool'.

Travellers from wholesale firms call in some parts of the country and buying from them needs special care. Some of the stock shown may be old and there is also a danger of duplication, as the same books may have been ordered from the publishers, but wholesalers are very useful people and, used intelligently, save the bookseller time and money. Some paperback wholesalers provide a more rapid service than the publishers.

When the publisher's representative sends the order through to his firm, the stock which is already published will be promptly dispatched and the new books will usually arrive *before* publication date. It is important to remember that books not only should *not be sold* before publication date, but should not be *exposed for sale*; nor must any display be made before then, even though the books are not actually supplied to the customer until the day of publication. A moment's reflection will show the wisdom of this, and every bookseller should, in the interests of the trade, conform with the arrangement. The whole idea of the publication date is to allow the publisher time to get copies to all bookshops in time for the day of publication. It is not possible to dispatch them all at once, and it follows that some booksellers will have supplies before others. If the booksellers first obtaining supplies display them they have the advantage over their fellows. The publication date is usually printed on the invoice and sometimes on the outside of the parcel. In the event of a bookseller making a mistake and showing the books in advance of publication, he should withdraw them immediately the mistake is discovered. It was once common practice for fellow booksellers to draw attention to any books exposed for sale before publication date, and to some extent this still applies, but, alas, all too frequently booksellers do not appear to observe publication date and if the system breaks down the smaller bookseller will be the loser as the larger buyers tend to get stock first.

To sum up, orders are mainly of two types:

(a) *Travellers' Orders*
    These orders given to a publisher's representative when he calls on the booksellers cover subscription (i.e. pre-publication) and stock orders. It is customary to hand such orders to the representative, who will send or take them to his office. Booksellers are strongly advised to keep a copy for their own reference and should number and date the order so that the publisher can quote it on his invoice.

(b) *Direct Orders*

These cover repeat orders for stock, subscription orders for books not yet published or orders from customers for books not in stock sent direct to the publisher. As regards 'Urgency of Orders' every publisher does his best to clear his orders as quickly as possible. Although in special cases he may be prepared to deal with an order out of turn, dealing with orders otherwise than strictly in rotation tends to disrupt his system and cause delay. However, so many booksellers mark their orders 'Urgent' (some even print the word on all their forms) that it has ceased to have much meaning. It is clearly impossible to give priority to them all. General practice is to give first place to orders sent by long-distance telephone, telegram, express post or some other relatively expensive medium, and to those orders where some good reason is given, as 'required for school prize-giving next Saturday', 'customer leaving the country', etc. Notice to the publisher of the *required date of delivery* will help him to decide by which means to dispatch. Orders sent in confirmation of telephone calls, etc., should be clearly marked as such. Experience shows that a publisher's post on Monday is usually three times the size of that on any other day. Orders posted by a bookseller in the first three days of the week, therefore, and arriving at the publisher's on Wednesday, Thursday and Friday are likely to be supplied more quickly. Early posting of orders in sealed envelopes at letter rates speeds up delivery. It is the policy of the Post Office not to release second-class mail until all first-class mail has been cleared (even if the publisher calls to collect it and it has been sorted).

Posting of Orders

Orders may be sent by two principal methods:

(a) *To the Publishers Direct*

This is a quick method, particularly if first-class rather than second-class post is used.

(b) *To the Publishers via Orders Clearing or Booksellers Order Distribution (BOD)*
These are the most economical ways and in the case of London publishers involve very little loss of time. Both perform the function of distributing the individual publishers orders sent in bulk by the booksellers. The bookseller sends all his orders in one envelope to Orders Clearing or BOD, where they are sorted and forwarded to the publishers (see page 207 for complete details of Orders Clearing and page 193 for BOD).

When more than one order form is sent to the same firm, they should be securely stapled together so that they can be executed as one order in one parcel or consignment. This helps the publisher and may reduce the carriage bill of the bookseller.

Essential Information

The following information is essential on any order form:

(a) *Name and address* of the bookseller, including the Postal Code. This should be clearly stated at the top. In the case of smaller towns the county should be given also.
(b) *Special instructions*, such as charging requests and delivery instructions, if required, should be clearly stated at the top of the form. Any further information or special instruction, such as 'On Sale', 'See Safe', etc., should also be given here.
(c) *Name of the publisher*. Although the address is not necessary, such abbreviations as CUP, OUP, UTP, ULP, etc., should be avoided, particularly when using Orders Clearing or BOD. They are easily misread and may cause error and delay.
(d) *Date* of order, *which should also be the actual date of posting* so that the publisher can keep a check on undue delays in receipt of orders.
(e) *Name of carrier* or method of dispatch is required. Since many publishers now send part or all of their parcels carriage free

(and therefore use what methods suit them best), it is best to state: 'send per —— if not carriage paid'.

(f) *Order numbers*, boldly shown at the top of the form, kept as brief as possible to avoid transcription mistakes. They are of help in the subsequent identification of invoices or in the event of queries.

(g) *Number of copies required*. This number should be written clearly in figures. The use of such terms as '½ doz.' or 'gross', etc., should be avoided, and if a reference number is used by the bookseller against each line of his order it should be kept quite separate to avoid confusion with the quantity. The numbering of each line of an order is also liable to cause the dispatch of the wrong quantity. The quantity is best shown to the left of the title. Special care is necessary when ordering series; for example, if four copies are wanted of each of four titles in a series, the number of copies, as always, should be shown on each line of the order.

(h) *Author and Title* of books required, as explicit as possible, details of price (which, even if out of date, helps in identification), and name of series if there is likely to be doubt about the edition required. In the case of the Bible, Prayer Books, etc., the publisher's catalogue number must be used to ensure that the right edition is supplied. Each title should be on a separate line, even if several titles are part of a series. Ordering by series numbers should be avoided where possible unless encouraged by the publisher. Publishers should themselves avoid using Roman numerals in series numbers. Where multi-volume books are available as complete sets or in parts, booksellers should clearly state what is required; parts should be ordered on separate lines. For books published with or without answers (e.g. mathematical books) the edition required should be clearly indicated. Also quote binding, hardback or paperback or colour, etc., when titles are available in several editions. In case of doubt quote the ISBN number.

(i) *Increases on previous orders or cancellation of orders* should give full particulars, for example, 'increase my O/N 7 of 25.4.73 from 6 to 12 copies of ——'. In the case of increase it is better to place a new order rather than amend an order previously given.

Brevity and Clarity

Orders should be kept as brief as possible and the Standard Order Form is recommended. *Badly written orders cause delay* and often have to be referred back to the sender, with consequent waste of time.

Other Points to Remember when Ordering

Queries, requests for publicity material, extra jackets, etc., should *not* be included on order forms but sent on separate sheets. Similarly cheques in payment of accounts should not be attached or referred to on any order. Such matters normally involve a separate department of the publisher and the same piece of paper cannot be dealt with simultaneously in both departments.

Orders should be legible and preferably typed. Clerks in publishing houses waste more time puzzling over indecipherable orders than on any other part of their job, and such orders lead to error. Make sure your order clerk sends the order to the correct publisher (especially in the case of publishers with similar names). Publishers receiving other publishers' orders do not always pass them on (even to Orders Clearing).

Methods of Dispatch

A publisher consigns his books either carriage free or carriage forward. In the former case, the choice of carrier is his; in the latter, the bookseller must choose and state his choice *on each order*. It is not sufficient to give general instructions such as 'always send my parcels by post'. A publisher may have many thousands of accounts, and orders on which no carrier is shown are subject to delay while the information is being found. A bookseller's choice of carrier is wide and he will have to balance cost against speed of delivery. The principal methods are:

(a) *Post*. This is probably the quickest, but also the most expensive method.

(b) *Carriers*. There are various carriers and forwarding agents who will accept parcels for onward dispatch. BRS and Atlas give nation-wide coverage. Services and costs vary widely. Booksellers should choose the carrier who is best for their area.

(c) *Rail*. This is little used by booksellers. Passenger train is quick in areas with frequent rail services but can be erratic in others. It is costly, so when speed is essential post is usually more convenient. Some publishers have special flat-rate arrangements with the railways.

(d) *Publishers and Booksellers Parcels Delivery Service (PPDS)*. The PPDS is a specialized distribution service for the book trade, set up by Book Centre Ltd, at the request of the Publishers and Booksellers Associations. It aims to give booksellers a very fast and efficient delivery service at a very low cost to publishers. The service covers the whole of the United Kingdom and the Republic of Ireland and may be extended to the Continent. PPDS has the advantage of being an organization set up solely for the book trade with regular and reliable delivery times to all booksellers. It is able to make emergency arrangements to ensure continuity of communication between publisher and booksellers in time of national crisis, such as during the postal strike of 1971. With depots and a network of trunking routes covering the United Kingdom, deliveries are made daily, twice or three times a week to all booksellers, depending on the volume of traffic. Costs are generally lower than other services and vary, depending upon quantity and weight. Details can be obtained from Book Centre Ltd, North Circular Road, Neasden, London NW10 0JE. (See page 204.)

In case of special urgency or for some other reason a bookseller may request that a book be sent *direct* to his customer. In such cases he should send a separate order with his own addressed label attached, stating on the order his customer's name and

Order

From:

To:

ALWAYS QUOTE
Order No. 48768

Date:

BOOKSELLER'S ACCOUNT NO.

IF POSSIBLE, RETURN YELLOW COPY ORDER WITH BOOKS AND/OR REPORTS

CONSIGN TO, IF DIFFERENT ADDRESS:

SPECIAL INSTRUCTIONS:

CUSTOMER'S REF.	QTY	ISBN	SERIES, AUTHOR, TITLE	CLOTH, PAPER OR PRICE	PUB. USE

Specimen of Standard Order Form   (Actual size, $8\frac{1}{4} \times 5\frac{1}{4}$ in.)

address in case there should be any subsequent query. Publishers generally will not hold themselves responsible for any losses which may occur when books are sent direct to a bookseller's customer. It is a matter of law that ownership of goods which are sent carriage forward is transferred from the sender to the consignee at the moment of dispatch, although any claims for losses on the carrier may have to be made through the publishers as consignees on behalf of the bookseller. Moreover, publishers who normally pay carriage will usually charge it to the bookseller if sending books direct, and publishers may in any case place a limit on the number of special dispatches they are prepared to make for any one account.

Reminders

Reminders given to publishers by booksellers of orders not yet received should:

(a) Be clearly marked 'Claim' or 'Reminder Only', to avoid duplication.

(b) Be on a separate piece of paper and not on an order or statement of account.

(c) Contain the date, number of the order and other relevant details to which they refer.

Dust Jackets

Within limits, if stock is available, publishers are usually prepared to supply fresh jackets to replace torn or soiled ones in a book-seller's stock. This is best arranged on a representative's call. If ordered direct from a publisher the bookseller should ensure that the order is clearly marked, 'Jacket Only'.

Do's and Don'ts for Booksellers

Orders

Do ensure that your order form is of a reasonable size and not too flimsy. *The Standard Order Form* is recommended.

Do remember that the publisher has to add a lot of information to the order, and leave him plenty of blank space at the foot and both sides of the order form.

Do type your order or, if this is impossible, make a special effort to write clearly.

Do send a duplicate copy if you want the original order returned.

Do ensure that the following information is clearly stated:

(a) Your own name and address.
(b) The publisher's name.
(c) The date of the order.
(d) Your own order number.
(e) The correct title and, if possible, the price, using a separate line for each title even when part of a series.
(f) Whether the hardback or paperback edition is required, when both are available.
(g) Any special instructions, for example, 'On Sale'.

Do use a separate order form for publicity material, jackets, queries, etc.

Do send your own label if you want the publisher to dispatch books direct to your customer.

Do restrict 'Urgent' orders to cases of genuine need which should be explained. Use a separate order form.

Do mark reminders clearly to avoid duplication and do not include them in an order.

Do remember that, if you have more than one order, to send via Orders Clearing or Booksellers Order Distribution. Use the cheapest methods.

Receipt of Goods

Do check goods against the invoice or advice note as soon as this is received and notify the publisher at once if there are any discrepancies.

Do quote the publisher's invoice number and date in any correspondence about a delivery.

Do give a qualified signature for a parcel that appears to have been opened or damaged.

Returns (see also pages 48–54)

Don't return books other than damaged or imperfect, or books sent 'See Safe' or 'On Sale', without first getting the publisher's approval.

Do NOT include any order with parcels.

Do include an advice note with all returns, giving the following information:

(a) Your name and address.

(b) A list of the books included in the consignment and the number and dates of the invoices on which they were supplied.

(c) Whether you require credit or exchange.

(d) Why the books have been returned; for example, imperfect, order duplicated, etc.

Do ensure that books returned are in mint condition and properly packed.

Do use Standard Order Forms, Publishers' Returns Labels and any address label provided by publishers.

5

Trade Terms

As I said earlier bookselling is full of problems which have been debated by both booksellers and publishers over the years, and although some of the problems are not now as pressing, many are no nearer being resolved, including the most thorny of all— 'publishers' terms', which (at the risk of labouring the point) are not only insufficient but unnecessarily complicated.

The late Mr Frank Sanders, a former Secretary of the Publishers Association and late Managing Director of Book Centre Ltd, wrote in *The Bookseller* (26 October 1968): 'One of the most chaotic aspects of the book trade is represented by publishers' terms. Every publisher has his own set of terms and terms are used as sales and competitive factors. But several examinations of publishers' terms in recent years (made in conjunction with ill-fated attempts to rationalize terms) have shown that basically the publishers' bewildering variety of terms can be placed into four or five groups. This must mean that variations in terms are devices with which it is hoped to lead the bookseller into buying more than he would otherwise do. Is there, however, now any evidence that the bookseller falls for this sort of thing? And, if not, why not drop this device in favour of a plain and rationalized set of terms and thus save much time in their calculations and checking?'

A most difficult problem also arises from the single-copy order. In no other trade is the retailer expected to order one single item to meet the demand of a particular customer, irrespective of price, but the customer in a good bookshop expects such a service, and that free. It must be obvious that where a bookseller orders a low-priced book to meet a special order he must do so at a loss, as the order and postage on it must be paid for and the publisher is likely to charge the cost of postage, so, without taking time into consideration, the transaction will cost the bookseller a good deal more than he will receive. What is not appreciated by the book-buying public is that a loss is often made, or at least no profit made, when a single copy of a book costing as much perhaps as £1.50 is specially ordered. The bookseller bears the cost of postage or carriage to him, plus the original cost of ordering by order form or telephone call, and there are other overheads such as the assistant's time. In fairness it must be appreciated that the looking-out, invoicing and packing of books frequently results in a financial loss to the publisher too; so a few charge a service fee on low-value orders, or one way or another make the bookseller pay more for the book by giving lower terms for a single copy or by passing on the cost of postage or carriage. Some publishers would argue that the book-seller might well pass on such charges to his customers; and the bookseller would probably reply that his competitors do not do so and he cannot risk losing goodwill. The Book Trade Working Party agreed that 'in principle, all service and carriage charges should be discontinued. If a low value order charge has to be imposed it should be standardized', and no bookseller would disagree with that.

Both booksellers and publishers tend to be individualists, and this is both the strength and weakness of the trade, but it does often complicate matters. For instance, publishers' terms of supply vary so greatly that no bookseller can remember them, so if, for instance, by ordering two copies or more a bookseller could get better terms he must frequently spend valuable time finding out.

Publishers' trade terms are varied to the point where they border on the ridiculous and need a special directory to list them. *A Directory of Publishers* published by the Booksellers Association gives full particulars of the terms of each publisher listed and a handy, quick reference called *Handbook of Selected*

Publishers' Terms is also available. The latter is a booklet published by the Charter Group of the Booksellers Association.

These books, used intelligently, can save the bookseller a considerable amount of money, but even reference to these takes up valuable time.

The Publishers Association in its *Book Distribution Handbook* concludes, 'the rationalization of publishers' terms is long overdue. Life for a bookseller would be much simpler if this were done. Efforts have been and will continue to be made to bring this about but in the meantime the only generalization is that discounts are better for general books than for educational books.' In a joint statement by the Councils of the Booksellers Association and the Publishers Association on the Book Trade Working Party Report, 1972,[1] it was 'jointly agreed that much simplification of procedures in the book trade is desirable, and that this particularly applies to the terms on net books. The PA Council, however, is not free, for legal and constitutional reasons, to hold any views on this or to issue any general directive regarding the level of discounts.' The Working Party had proposed a standard discount on all net books.

The BA Council unilaterally endorsed the Working Party's

[1] The Book Trade Working Party was brought into being at the 1970 Booksellers Conference. Its terms of reference were:

To establish the economic requirements of a prosperous and continuing home book trade capable of ensuring the widest availability of all kinds of books to the potential book-buying public, including specific consideration of the following:

1 An analysis of the profitability of general, academic and specialist bookselling and recommendations to improve their economic viability.
2 A review of the effects of the Net Book Agreement on bookselling profitability and book distribution, including the impact of new methods of trading.
3 Direct purchasing by local authorities.
4 Methods of increasing the amount of public money spent on book purchasing by local authorities, institutions, and students.

The BTWP was to report its findings (with immediate reports on matters of urgency) to the Councils of the two Associations, together with any recommendations for action which the BTWP might consider desirable to enable the industry to operate profitably and effectively. An interim report was to be submitted for circulation to the membership of the two Associations. A report was published in 1972.

opinion that there should be a minimum trade discount of 35 per cent, carriage paid, on all net books, while adding that such a minimum should not preclude booksellers with special claims to efficiency from securing additional bonus terms.

✼✼✼✼✼✼✼✼✼✼✼✼✼✼✼✼✼✼✼✼✼✼✼✼✼✼✼✼✼✼✼✼✼✼✼✼✼

6

Receipt of Books and Returns to Publishers

How many books wrongly supplied find their way into a book-seller's stock? Publishers can make mistakes and any well-run business checks incoming goods with the order book. All too frequently there is no indication on a publisher's invoice when books are supplied 'On Sale or Return'. There is, therefore, a possibility that the invoices will be accepted and passed for payment as if they were firm orders. The following procedure is recommended:

Receipt of Parcels

When parcels are received by a bookseller they should be checked to include the following points:

(a) Check the number of parcels to ensure that only the number delivered are signed for.

(b) Examine the parcels for damage, and if they appear likely to have been tampered with, sign for them as 'unexamined'.

(c) Contents of parcels must be checked against the Invoice/ advice note and the original order(s). Losses or damage which appear to have been caused in transit should be notified to the publisher forthwith, giving full details of invoice number(s) and date(s), details of discrepancies and/or damage, method of carriage, date of delivery, and whether or not the signature given was qualified.

(d) Damage through indifferent packing or publishers' errors should be dealt with as returns (see pages 51–2).

(e) When books are sound, and in accord with the invoice and order, they should be checked for price. In the case of net books, the prices shown on the invoice should be the same as those printed on the books; should there be a discrepancy, the retail price given on the invoice is the correct one, and the publisher should be notified of the discrepancy.

(f) The invoice must pass through the order department so that orders can be cleared, dues recorded for future progress and customers notified of dues or inability to supply.

(g) The invoice can be passed to the accounts department for payment.

(h) In the case of carriage-forward parcels any losses or damage in transit must be reported to carriers within three days, as the consignee is responsible for claims against the carriers. Carriage-forward arrangements to booksellers are to be discouraged, as they involve additional work for both carrier and bookseller.

Many booksellers have discarded a system which was in common practice years ago, but it can be still used in smaller shops, that is, to mark in each book the cost price (in code) and the published price, unless the latter appeared, as it usually did, on the jacket. This cost price in code can be useful at stocktaking time, depending on the method used, and often also serves the purpose of helping to identify stolen books. For stocktaking purposes it is advisable to include with the code some registration letter which will indicate when the book was purchased. For instance, 1/73 might indicate that the book was bought in January 1973; 3/73 that the book was bought in March 1973. It is still useful to know the age of stock and this can be done by the very simple system of using a letter of the alphabet for each six-monthly period, starting with the letter *A* for all stock purchased in the first six months of the financial year, *B* for the second six months, *C* for the first six months of the following year and so on.

A soft pencil should be used when making any marks in books; on no account should an indelible or hard pencil be used, or books will be disfigured. Exercise of common sense is necessary in all markings of books; for instance, to write a cost on the black end-paper of a Holy Bible is certain to disfigure it, and in many instances coloured end-papers are unsuitable for marking. Customers usually like to be able to erase bookseller's marks. The first fly-leaf generally seems to be a good position for the noting of cost marks, etc., but some booksellers prefer to use the inside of the back cover.

If it is desired to put a cost price in code in books it is not difficult to find a word or series of letters suitable for a code. In the case of a word, the obvious essential is to have one in which no letters are duplicated. Perhaps the commonest is:

$$\begin{array}{cccccccccc} C & U & M & B & E & R & L & A & N & D \\ 1 & 2 & 3 & 4 & 5 & 6 & 7 & 8 & 9 & 10 \end{array}$$

A variation is for the letter *D* to indicate 0 (nil); or a further letter is required to indicate nil, for example *X*. Using this code 35p could be written /*ME*; and £5.50 would be *E/EX*.

When the books are marked they are put into stock, except those which have to wait for a later publication date. These are kept on one side, the top copy having protruding from it a slip of paper giving the date of publication, so that the books will be brought forward into stock at the right time without delay.

Imperfect Copies

In the case of imperfections in books priced at less than £1.50 many publishers will automatically give credit or exchange on receipt of the torn-out title-page annotated to show the nature of the imperfection. The ceiling price varies, so check with the Directory of British Publishers. The rest of the book should be retained for at least one month in case the publisher, printer or binder needs to examine it. In the case of books priced £1.50 or over the book should be retained intact and the imperfection reported to the publisher so that he may decide how best to deal with it. The Booksellers Association includes a list of publishers who accept annotated title-pages of imperfect copies, and their price limits, in The Directory of British Publishers. The publisher will, of course, claim on the printer or binder under arrangements made with the Publishers Association and the British Federation of Master Printers.

Duplication of Orders

If an order has been duplicated, the bookseller returning the surplus book(s) should give the publisher full particulars (i.e. the dates and numbers of both invoices). Duplication of orders may often occur because a representative has unwittingly subscribed the same book twice and the last order has not been marked CPO (cancel previous order). The other main cause of duplication is an excess of zeal on the part of the publisher to satisfy his customer. A bookseller may query the non-receipt of an order shortly after its dispatch, and when it is in the publisher's 'pipeline' it may be extremely difficult and time-consuming to check. If it cannot be traced a duplicate parcel may be dispatched to ensure that the bookseller receives the book.

Returns to Publishers (see also page 43)

These can be classified under two headings:

(a) Books which can be returned without the prior consent of the publisher and comprise:

   (i) Books which have been supplied in error or have been damaged in transit.

   (ii) The balance of orders received 'see safe', 'on sale', 'on consignment' or 'on approval'.

(b) Books which require the prior consent of the publishers before they are returned. These comprise:

   (i) *Duplicated orders*

   (ii) *Overstocks*

     If a bookseller is unable to sell a complete purchase of books from a publisher he may wish to return some of the books and obtain credit for them. These are 'overstocks'.

Use the Standard Return Form

In all cases the specially designed Returns Form will facilitate the procedure for the return of books and reduce clerical work to a minimum. The form is available from, and prices will be supplied on application to, the Booksellers Association. A specimen of this form is reproduced on page 55.

Publishers' Returns Labels

Where books are being returned without prior consent of the publisher because they have been supplied in error or have been damaged in transit, it is advisable to use the green 'Returns Label' obtainable from the Publishers Association. This should be affixed to the outside of the parcel. It indicates that the books are being returned because of defect or because they do not conform to the original order and ensures that the publisher gives priority to these returns. The parcel must contain documents (preferably the Standard Return Form) giving details of the bookseller and reasons for return.

Dispatch of Parcels of Returns

Parcels must be returned carriage paid. In cases where they are being returned because of a publishers' error, the cost of the carriage can be claimed from the publisher. It is, however, worth noting that even if a publisher admits such a claim, he will frequently only credit the cost of the carriage by the cheapest possible means. In this connection, whilst booksellers are at liberty to use any means they wish to send the parcel, it is worth noting the most convenient and the cheapest method for any sizeable parcel at present is the returns service of Publishers' and Booksellers' Parcels Delivery Service (PPDS), fully explained on pages 53-4. Prepaid labels can be obtained from PPDS, Book Centre Ltd, PO Box 30, Neasden, London NW10 0JE, and should be affixed to the parcel in addition to any other labels supplied by the publisher, etc.

Publishers' and Booksellers' Parcels Delivery Service

The main objects of this Returns Scheme are to speed the return of books and simplify administration and accounting. To this end a returns label has been devised and PPDS drivers on their normal rounds accept parcels showing this label. Drivers will not collect parcels without the returns label on them. Any question of payment for carriage for authorized or non-authorized returns is not the responsibility of PPDS and must be taken up by booksellers with publishers direct. This applies to all publishers, even those for whom Book Centre warehouse and distribute.

Procedure

Booksellers who wish to use the service are asked to comply with the following procedure in order to ensure that their parcels reach their destination with a minimum of delay.

(a) Each parcel for return should be packed in a substantial carton and have one returns label, which has been completed in detail, affixed to the outside of the carton. If the parcels contain 'publishers' errors' then a green errors label will also be necessary, as now.

(b) In addition, the bookseller is required to complete a list, *in duplicate*, which contains the following information:
   (i) Name and address of the bookseller returning the parcel.
   (ii) The serial number of the returns label.
   (iii) Name and address of the publisher to whom the parcel is to be dispatched.[1]
   (iv) Date of collection by the PPDS driver.

The reason for the list and the information it contains is to enable the PPDS service to give proof of delivery on these parcels. Any queries on non-delivery should be addressed to the Claims Section, PPDS Book Centre Ltd, PO Box No. 30, North Circular Road, Neasden, London, NW10 0JE, where they will be processed in

[1] Labels must be addressed to Book Centre, Southport, or Book Centre, Denham, whichever is appropriate. Ascertain from Book Centre which publishers' returns are handled in each of these two centres.

accordance with the RHA conditions of carriage. The PPDS drivers have been instructed to accept only parcels which bear the returns label and are accompanied by the detailed list explained above. The driver will sign both lists, retain one copy and ask the bookseller to retain the duplicate. The returns parcels can be handed to the driver when he is making a delivery. PPDS regret that it will not be possible to call at booksellers solely for the collection of returns parcels.

The scheme applies only to booksellers who receive their deliveries by PPDS vans.

1. REQUEST TO RETURN

Always QUOTE

To ....

From ....

....

Listed by ....

Where applicable quote:—

Bookseller's Order number	
Publisher's Invoice number	
Publisher's Invoice date	

Date permission requested ....

Date books returned ....

Permission Granted

Signed ....

for Publisher

If permission to return is granted, publisher need only sign this request and return pages 1 and 2 to the bookseller. He keeps page 3.

Please may we return the books listed below, for the reasons given:

Quantity	Publisher's use (ISBN)	Author	Title	Retail Price	Reason Code	Pub. use (Discount)	For Publisher's use only

Permission from publisher needed for reason (a), (b) and (c) and perhaps (m)

(a) Order duplicated by us
(b) Recommended textbook that has been dropped
(c) Customer cancelled order
(d) In perfect

(e) Received damaged
(f) Wrong title/edition supplied
(g) From "on sale/on approval"
(h) Duplication by you

(i) As arranged with representative/by letter
(j) Old edition, exchange for new edition
(k) Recalled by publisher

(m) Other reason

7

Display and Stock Arrangement

Stock in a bookshop should be so arranged that it is presented in the way most likely to obtain maximum sales, and at the same time it must be so arranged that any member of the staff, and as far as possible the shopping public, will know where to look for a particular title.

Display, therefore, often conflicts with order, so some compromise is necessary. Ideally all books in stock would best be face-displayed, but that is impossible as lack of space prevents this. Again, books in the window or on display tables or stands are often divorced from their classifications on the shelves, so are books in series such as the Everyman's Library or World's Classics. These are usually kept together in the series and not in classifications into which the individual titles could go. So it is important for a bookseller to find the best place for each title and for each classification in his shop.

Where there is a large stock it seems little short of miraculous to an uninitiated customer that the bookseller is able, immediately, to go to a table or shelf and find the books asked for.

There is, of course, some order in almost every bookshop, and good booksellers have the bulk of their stock carefully classified, with perhaps a few tables containing the latest books, where classification may not be exact. Books are usually kept on the shelves in their correct classification under the author's name, and it is unwise to have large stocks, even on display tables, without some arrangement or classification. Nothing is more infuriating than to refuse an order for a book and afterwards find it in stock. The chance to sell it may not recur, and even if it does, one sale is possibly lost, as the second customer might well have been prepared to wait for a copy if the bookseller had not reordered one for stock.

It is a common practice in the best bookshops to have sections clearly marked. In large shops this is done by means of notices at the top of bookcases, smaller sections being indicated by means of narrow printed slips fixed to the front edges of the shelves. Classifications must obviously vary in accordance with the nature of the business. The more general ones include Fiction (which may be subdivided into Novels, Light Romance, Thrillers and Detective Stories, Westerns); Children's Books (commonly subdivided into age groups and sometimes into subjects such as Nature Books, Religion, Careers, History, etc.); and non-fiction for adults, classified under, for example, Gardening, Cookery, Nature, History, Topography, Literature, Religion, Biography, Travel, Maps and Guides, Economics, Technical, Medical. Other classifications will readily suggest themselves.

The Children's Section

Every bookseller, even the specialist, can with advantage have a section of books for children. The selling of children's books has become more important to the trade year by year. Large bookshops which at one time stocked hardly any children's books today have separate sections or even large departments devoted entirely to children's books all the year round. Children's books now sell throughout the year, whereas in the past they often had only a Christmas sale in some bookshops. Their sale is still largely seasonal in some multiple shops, stores, stationers' and newsagents', particularly in establishments which do not regularly stock books but have quantities of Annuals, Rewards and Bumper Books on sale in the Christmas season. In spite of such competition booksellers have, by careful selection of really worth-while books, built up a steady business, and the children's section attracts adults and young people alike.

The selling of children's books is one of the most delightful aspects of bookselling and of greater importance to the future of a business than might at first be thought. Once the book-buying and reading habit is formed in a child, it is fairly certain that on reaching mature years he will retain the habit, with the possibility that the custom will be continued in the shop where, in childhood days, books were bought. The children's books will bring in many a parent wishing to buy books for birthdays and other presents, and there is always the chance that other books will be purchased at the same time.

However small a shop, the inclusion of a children's section is therefore recommended. The stock throughout the year need not be large, but it is advisable for the bookseller to buy a selection of the important new publications as they are issued, particularly in the Autumn. A really useful range of children's books can be maintained with little risk, as many favourite books for children continue to sell year after year. Selection for stock from the enormous range of new books is not an easy matter, but good print and good illustrations are most important. There are many publishers who specialize in the production of children's books and several of them have long experience, so it is perhaps wise for buyers with little experience to deal with these. It must in fairness be admitted, however, that several fairly new publishers are producing some of the best books for children.

Rag-books, cardboard cut-out books and painting books all come within the range of the children's book section. Even with these, quality is important, and to build up a high-class book business it is necessary to buy only the best. Standard works are as necessary in the children's section as in the adults'. The bookseller should not hesitate, therefore, to buy some of the more expensive books with really first-class illustrations by well-known illustrators. Adults, when buying for children, can be discriminating and show a marked preference for the best production. They are not usually attracted by children's books which are in any way 'horrific', either in text or in illustrations, but children appear to like them and, after all, some of the favourite classics such as *Snow White*, *Hansel and Gretel*, or *The Water*

Babies, to mention a few, are grim and sad. *Struwwelpeter* is 'too much' for many adults.

Whether serving an adult or a child with a book, the bookseller should try to sell one which will give pleasure. When adults seek the bookseller's guidance in selecting books for children, he has a serious duty, as the choice may well have an influence on the reading habits and even on the character of a child. Considered in this way, a responsibility rests on the bookseller which must never be abused.

It seems correct to assume that children of today are more independent generally than those of former years. Modern education encourages greater freedom of thought and action, and domestic conditions no longer entail the young person being accompanied by an adult on his or her shopping expeditions, as was often the case with children of past generations. Therefore we get children coming into bookshops alone to choose for themselves or select books as presents for friends. This shopping by children makes it important that the shelves of books in the children's section should be placed within easy reach and at the eye-level of the average child, so that he can make his choice without constantly demanding help. The assistant, however, should be alert to give advice when needed and should show the same interest, courtesy and friendliness as when attending an adult. This is most important.

Book Tokens (see Chapter 17) have the effect of bringing children into the bookshops, particularly after Christmas, to exchange the tokens which they have received as presents. It is always a delight to have these happy youngsters in the shop, and booksellers who make them welcome to such a degree that they have no fear of entering a shop are serving the book trade and the child well. Let the children pick over the books but keep a watchful eye on them and, if they handle books so carelessly that they are damaging them, they can be gently instructed in the correct way of 'looking' at books. Children do like being allowed to select their own books, and the bookseller can learn more from the children than from the parents about the books he should buy for them, if he will patiently observe and listen to these young buyers.

As there are so many current titles in juvenile literature it is advisable to divide the stock into sections: books for boys and girls, and perhaps into age-groups—books for young children and books for older boys and girls—as well as into subjects, such as books on Animals, Sports, Hobbies, Poetry and Religion. A section of Children's Classics is also important; many of the well-known cheap pocket editions and paperbacks contain titles that are great favourites, especially with older children. Toddlers' books and picture books can be displayed separately to advantage. In this way selection is made much easier both for children and for the bewildered adults helping them.

✤✤

8

Selling and Sales Staff

Several famous bookselling businesses have been built up by the personality of the booksellers, their knowledge and enthusiasm for good literature, their bibliographical knowledge, attention to detail, charm and power to make customers feel at home and their selling ability. To this day the selling of books ranks with the highest intellectual pursuits, and good salesmanship entails much more in bookselling than in many other forms of retailing.

The primary requisite of all booksellers is knowledge, based on experience. This knowledge must include a mass of bibliographical detail, coupled with a thorough grounding in English Literature, a reasonable acquaintance with foreign literature, and an exact knowledge of the contents and use of reference books. A bookseller who reads a great deal is bound to be more knowledgeable than one who reads but rarely, but it does not follow that he will be a better businessman. Some compromise is necessary between erudition and commercialism, but to a bookseller all knowledge is useful—'a little learning' far from being 'a dangerous thing' is often a great asset in bookselling. There is joy in bookselling and tremendous satisfaction in living with books, in meeting the people who write them, publish them, and, best of all, buy them. All good booksellers and publishers have a professional interest in their work and do not judge everything purely on an economic basis.

Inexperienced assistants often do not realize the opportunities they have missed and may feel they are doing well by making the occasional substitute suggestion when a book is not in stock or is out of print. So far so good, of course! But it is possible to increase sales materially by subtle suggestion selling along more general lines. This must not be confused with 'pushing' sales; the use of such methods as those of, say, a hairdresser forcing hair creams or shaving soap upon an unwilling customer drives customers away. Customers must never be irritated or embarrassed. The art is to introduce books that the customer is really delighted to see, and it is obvious that the ability to do this can be acquired only by wide reading and sound judgement. One can always be more convincingly enthusiastic about a book one has read (or at least partly read) with enjoyment.

As there are essential differences between the selling of books and the selling of other goods, it is not sufficient for a textbook on bookselling to list the virtues required by every salesman, such as patience, tact, the understanding of people, character, integrity, enthusiasm, and so on, and to analyse successful methods of selling. There exist in any case plenty of books on salesmanship. It is more necessary to dwell in some detail on essential points which are vital to good bookselling, though it is true many may be applied equally to salesmanship generally. This matter is summed up under the headings 'What to Do' and 'What Not to Do'.

What to Do

Conduct customers to the sections they ask for, and stay a moment or two to see if they require further assistance. An airy wave of the hand in a vague direction is not good bookselling. Neither is it tactful to stand stolidly by a customer and so possibly embarrass him. A good assistant must be able to distinguish between the independent, knowledgeable customers who prefer to browse on their own, and those who rely on him for guidance.

Acknowledge the presence of a customer who is waiting while a transaction with another is completed. A pleasant smile and 'I will not keep you a moment' should establish good relations from the start. A good assistant must not have a one-track mind, but must, on occasion, be alert to the needs of several customers at once while giving proper attention to each in turn. This is not an easy thing to do, but courtesy carries one a long way.

Always take the name and address when taking orders or inquiries either in the shop or over the telephone. Failure to take full particulars at the time may cause endless trouble later on.

Even in this permissive age customers are impressed if staff dress neatly and tidily and look businesslike.

Take especial care with difficult or complaining customers, and never allow one to walk out in a 'huff'. If you cannot give satisfaction call a superior to try to get the difficulty settled amicably.

Let the customer do at least some of the talking. He is probably more interested in airing his knowledge and opinions than in hearing yours.

Look up references in front of the customer instead of disappearing round a corner for some minutes. A customer will not find waiting tedious if he sees you are actively engaged in trying to trace a book for him. Reference books should be kept in an accessible place in the shop.

What Not to Do

Do not use trade terms or publishers' 'Answers', either in conversation or in writing, when they can be avoided. A bookseller should always know the exact meaning of trade terms and abbreviations, but the public cannot be expected to do so and some are rather misleading. 'Reprinting' for instance, often suggests that a book will be available again soon, but that may not be the case. (An up-to-date list of 'Publishers' Replies' with meanings appears in Appendix II on page 228.)

Do not lounge about, or on the other hand, be so occupied that you do not attend to a customer at once; lack of attention, even for a moment, can make a customer feel an unwelcome intruder and spoil a possible sale.

Do not stand chatting in groups in the shop. You may be talking business but it looks unbusinesslike.

Do not 'look too good, nor talk too wise'—advice that is

particularly applicable to bookshop assistants. Many people are
a little timid of bookshops and bookshop assistants. Assistants
can help and encourage such people by being careful not to ride
literary high horses.

Do not eat in view of the customers. Sweets, chewing gum,
lozenges, etc., should be consumed out of sight.

Do not hold long conversations with customers when others
are waiting, unless it is absolutely necessary. A skilful assistant
can tactfully break off a conversation without giving the slightest
offence.

Do not vary your courtesy and attention according to the
status, or assumed status, of the customer. There must be no
'best manners' for best customers, and less attention to unknown
or less smartly dressed ones. Clothes and grooming are no sure
guide to a customer's social status or bank balance.

Do not give the impression that the customer has asked for
something out of the way by facial expression or by such remarks
as, 'Oh, that's an old book!' or 'We never stock it, as there is no
demand for it here', and never say, 'Never heard of it!'

Do not take books back unless you first try to make certain
they were purchased in your shop and have not been read. If
you make exchange or cash refund too easy the courtesy will
be abused and some customers will use you rather like a lending
library. To avoid this I instruct staff to say, 'I will see the manager,'
when asked to accept back a book, particularly if a cash refund
is requested. This tends to check any abuse.

This list could be extended, but it will no doubt have served
to indicate some pitfalls and to show that booksellers must be
psychologists, sympathetic and approachable.

Assistants must have knowledge of the stock and its whereabouts. Customers are not favourably impressed if they see
assistants wandering about and searching in the wrong classifications, obviously not knowing where to look. A knowledge of
stock is gained not so much through the exercise of a good
memory, as by the degree of interest taken, plus a methodical
and regular scrutiny of the daily deliveries of new stock and a
constant study of stock on the shelves.

Book sales can be substantially increased by intelligent and skilled 'suggestion selling'. Some assistants are particularly good at this, and they are invaluable. There is all the difference between 'suggestion selling' and 'pushing' sales, to the embarrassment of the customer. Booksellers cannot over-sell by suggestion selling, and it will be found that customers will return again and again for their helpful guidance; but an aggressive salesman is definitely out of place in the good-class bookshop.

There are many ways in which a bookseller can exercise his imagination and initiative, but no aspect of the trade offers more scope for the exercise of these qualities than that of suggestion selling. It is distinctly a flair or intuition but, like so many so-called intuitions, it is not so much a gift as a result of experience in the technique of salesmanship combined with a knowledge of books. Suggestion selling is a pleasure in itself, not only on account of the extra business but also because of the satisfaction in the selling of good titles, some of which may long have been on the shelves.

Suggestion selling includes an extended use of that method of 'summing-up' mentioned earlier. When the title asked for is not in stock, it may transpire from a few questions that the customer is not specially anxious to obtain that particular book, but had seen it reviewed and thought it would please a friend for whom he wished to buy a birthday present. Here is an opportunity to introduce suitable alternatives, if there is a danger that a sale will otherwise be lost, as the customer will not wait for a copy of the book asked for to be ordered specially. All this requires tact, commonsense psychology, and a thorough knowledge of the stock.

Having sold a cheap book on a particular subject to a customer who does not appear to be in a hurry to leave, the bookseller may, perhaps, afford him extra pleasure and make his visit to the shop memorable by inviting him to look at a new and exquisite book on the same subject. The approach must be one that makes it obvious that such an invitation is made as a courtesy. There must be no attempt to press him to buy the book. Yet the showing of the 'special book' does in fact often lead to an extra sale since, of course, many people ultimately buy dozens of books on the same and allied subjects but not necessarily all at one time.

There is a feeling of triumph when a customer who came expecting to spend a few pence goes out with several pounds' worth of books and is delighted with his purchases, and there is great satisfaction, too, in those words of appreciation for courtesy, help and guidance which grateful customers from time to time bestow on helpful assistants.

Bookselling is a friendly trade, but, remember, it is a trade— you are not running a library or literary circle, so every sale counts.

Bookshop Assistants

We often hear it said that the book trade needs assistants of the right type, but the true meaning of 'right type' is not easy to arrive at. Some say that suitability is mainly a question of education, perhaps the possession of a university degree; others say a keen intelligence is what is required, with the ability to profit by experience. Others again couple appearance and charm of manner with these qualities. No doubt to some extent all these views are right, as the qualifications mentioned all count in the make-up of a promising assistant. Yet it does not follow that all candidates with these qualities have necessarily the makings of a good bookseller. Combined with other qualifications, they are an asset; but that elusive unidentifiable quality which seems to make a good bookseller out of a person who has no obvious qualifications is difficult to assess. It is certain that some of the more successful booksellers had, as youngsters, no outstanding educational or other qualifications. Some of them started in the trade straight from school, and by no means all had grammar-school educations. Few went to public school and still fewer to a university.

It would be foolish to deny that good education is an advantage, but it must be remembered that while one man is studying at the university, another is learning the trade in the bookshop. By the time the university student has a degree, the boy who started in the bookshop has learned a great deal about the business and has the advantage of practical experience. The door to bookselling should not be closed to young people who have not had a grammar-school education and do not possess formal qualifications; if it is, the book trade will lose much valuable material. Another point is that character will often succeed where intellectual achievement fails.

The selection of young entrants to bookselling is not easy, and the first few months' work is no sure guide. At some stage a real interest in the trade may be aroused, and an unpromising youngster may change almost overnight. This change may come about through the encouragement of a manager or even by that of a customer of long standing. A remark that gives an assistant the feeling that he really has in him the means to succeed can be most inspiring. Most of the older booksellers admit that the kindness, encouragement and thoughtfulness of customers had a real influence on their careers. Managers, under-managers and senior assistants too, can do much to encourage staff, and it is true to say that the future of the book trade is largely their responsibility.

The problem of staff is uppermost in the minds of those in the trade at the time of writing and is likely to remain so. Booksellers, publishers and customers alike complained of poor staff work when I wrote *The Truth about Bookselling*, but this is not so much the case today. Customers, particularly perhaps the more elderly ones, were not very tolerant of the young generation but I truly believe that gradually they are beginning to appreciate them, for many are bright, well-educated and keen. Perhaps we, in the book trade, are lucky, but in my experience today, as in the past, bookshop assistants do care and generally try hard to give good service.

Customers can be difficult at times, but in no circumstances must an assistant ever be rude, however provoked. Every assistant is actually representing his employer. It is impossible for an employer to serve every customer himself, and in the large organizations he may not have the time to serve any at all, so employs assistants to represent him. Seen in this light every assistant has an important function and status. Many newcomers to the trade, though they are excellent in other respects, need more knowledge, which can only be gained by longer experience, and too often customers complain that some of the courtesy they knew in the past is lacking; but here is a challenge for bookshop assistants so to improve matters by their attention and knowledge that they become recognized as outstanding in courtesy and service.

When engaging beginners, a bookseller would be wise to take them on for a long trial period, if possible. The trial period is obviously better than endeavouring to form an accurate judgement from one or two interviews and from testimonials which are not always reliable.

A new member of the staff must be a person who is likely to work well with the present members. Co-operation is vital if a bookshop is to run efficiently. Every assistant must be ready and willing to help others and to tackle, in an emergency, jobs which may ordinarily be done by someone else. Should a new-comer to the staff complain that he cannot get on with older members, one must of course invariably support the staff of long standing. If the newcomer really cannot get on with the others, it is far better for him to go elsewhere than cause any disharmony. At the same time, the proprietor must try to be absolutely just and be quite sure that any complaint of wrong treatment by any member of the staff is not dismissed without most careful consideration of all the relevant factors. The staff, particularly a large one, can perhaps be likened to a football team; each individual shines in certain positions but not in others —a good outside-left is not necessarily good in goal. Similarly each individual in a bookshop must, if not at once then later, be placed in the position for which he is best fitted, being moved if necessary as opportunity presents itself.

Stress is placed nowadays on vocational training of booksellers' assistants; the educational courses in various towns and the correspondence course arranged by the Booksellers Association have done much to stimulate interest and to help assistants of all ages. Assistants attending these classes or taking the courses have the benefit of instruction by booksellers who have long experience in the trade and who are often specialists in some section of it. But the bookseller and the bookshop manager can play the most important part in the training of staff during working hours. Their own enthusiasm and approach to bookselling are bound to influence the staff and be reflected in the business.

There are many practical ways of helping to train staff. In the first place, it is most important to have a plentiful supply of trade papers, preferably supplying one to each assistant for his own use. The importance of continuity of supply and having the papers immediately on publication cannot, surely, be over-estimated. The general practice, unfortunately, appears to be for a shop to take one copy, or at the most two, which the manager and senior assistant take home for the week-end or longer; it is then passed to the department for reference and must not be taken away. Consequently, many assistants enjoy no more than an occasional glimpse at trade papers in intervals of business, possibly some considerable time after publication. Merely to glance through trade papers is insufficient. They are filled with important news items and articles which are of great educational value and to deprive assistants of them is a short-sighted policy. It is suggested that every assistant should be given a free subscription to at least one trade paper, and that he should be asked to exchange papers with other assistants.

All newcomers to a bookshop staff, especially those with little or no previous experience, will feel strange and rather useless at first. It is advisable, therefore, to start them with some task that they can get on with by themselves, under the supervision of someone who will encourage and help them.

The importance of the daily first half-hour with the duster is often stressed quite rightly as a help in gaining knowledge of the books by handling them. This regular handling, tidying and display of stock, if undertaken intelligently and not as a mechanical duty, builds up in the mind a wealth of knowledge of books and is excellent for memory training. Newcomers to the trade should immediately begin to learn something of the contents of the shelves, and the sooner they fit into the daily routine and have certain duties and responsibilities of their own, the happier they are likely to be.

9

Display and Sales Promotion

It is often stated that many bookshops do not make the best use of one of the most successful methods of sales promotion at their disposal, namely the art of display, and particularly window display. Books lend themselves to most attractive forms of arrangement; and as the importance of display is universally acknowledged, it is a little difficult to discover why display does not, in bookselling, take the important place it does in retailing generally. In recent years both window and interior displays have improved but the trade has a long way to go to compete with the attention given to display by most other retailers.

There is no need to stress the sales appeal of a whole window given over to the display of a single title. In the larger bookshops this kind of display is often possible, but where it is not it is usually possible to focus attention on particular books or subjects by careful arrangement and suitable notices and sales aids.

The window is naturally of primary importance in attracting customers into the shop and it must therefore always be clean and tidy, well-lighted and as attractively arranged as possible. The glass itself must, of course, be clean and the stock dusted regularly. No faded notices or signs of neglect must be apparent. The window display may be said to reflect the whole service of the bookshop. Window displays should in part or in whole be changed weekly. If displays stay too long they lose impact and after a week the glass needs cleaning and the stock needs dusting.

To get best results window display should be the responsibility of one person who will then take an interest in it: it will be found that he improves by practice. Display must be encouraged by the manager who must take a true interest and give praise from time to time.

The planning of windows in advance is accepted as part of the routine in many branches of retail distribution, and booksellers are appreciating more and more the wisdom of planning and of giving special attention to display. Publishers will frequently oblige by sending stock on some returnable basis for a special display, and will usually provide free display material. Other local tradesmen are usually only too willing to lend articles which link up with particular books, such as pictures, some trellis-work for a gardening window, or a picnic hamper for a window of guides and maps. The possibilities are endless, and booksellers would find that this type of window display would not only sell the books in the window but would induce people interested in other books to come in and make inquiries. When borrowing articles, it is only courtesy to put in the window a small notice acknowledging the loan. This also serves to encourage other traders to lend articles, as not unnaturally they frequently benefit by obtaining sales for their goods so displayed.

As far as possible there should be, inside the shop, some link with the window display, for example a table or two of books on the same subject.

The seasons have obviously an important bearing on display; a window of gardening books in early spring when the ground is being prepared and the seeds sown will do better than a similar display in the winter. Books on the theatre, ballet and opera will do well in early winter, and books on travel and touring do best when people are making plans for their holidays.

The arrangement and display of books inside the shop is of no less importance than the display of those in the window; for instance, a table or two of religious books in Lent will attract attention where a window or part of a window cannot be devoted to them. There are many instances in which small interior displays are practicable. Such displays interest customers as they are, in a way, miniature exhibitions. A point to remember is that it is often advisable to continue a display inside the shop after it has been removed from the window, as the interest will probably be sustained for some time. A small table display of just one title can be most effective.

When book jackets get soiled or torn, the publishers usually provide fresh ones on request. When books have been handled rather freely they should be inspected, before return to stock, for thumb-marks on fly-leaves. These can usually be removed with a piece of indiarubber. Where valuable and beautiful books are displayed in such a way that the public handle them, soiling will be minimized if a tactful and tastefully produced reminder is included with the exhibit. A small notice, 'Please Handle with Care', or 'Fine Illustrated Books, Kindly Remove your Gloves', will not offend. Do not, however, overdo cautionary notices; they must never be large or vulgar. A gentle request usually commands most respect. In these days many booksellers wrap expensive art books in cellophane; this keeps them clean but has the disadvantage of having to be removed to enable a customer to examine the book. Nevertheless it is a system which has merit.

Familiar features of sales promotion for booksellers are authors' talks, children's book weeks, exhibitions, personal visits of celebrities to autograph copies of their books, literary luncheons and teas and, of course, catalogues, lists, prospectuses and advertisements. All these are excellent. They focus attention, create interest, stimulate trade and generally maintain and build up business. Authors' talks, if they are to be a success, should be restricted to those which are sure to interest customers. It is suggested that more literary gatherings could be held in the bookshops in the evenings. It would not be absolutely necessary to sell books at the time, but the author could sign copies for people attending the talk, and these copies could be bought and taken away the following day. Evening functions of this kind would, it is thought, make bookshops more of a rendezvous for book-lovers and create literary circles; it would also doubtless attract more customers into the bookshop.

School-teachers, parents and librarians will usually be most interested in children's book weeks, and will readily assist. The National Book League has much experience in this work, and is always ready to help and advise, and to provide material in a variety of ways.

Catalogues and other publicity material are dealt with later in this chapter, but every book sold can have a prospectus for another book or a copy of a book list slipped in by the salesman as the book is wrapped. A prospectus can be included from time to time when sending out accounts but care must be exercised as too regular inclusion can distract attention from the main purpose of sending the account, and hold up payment. Experience tends to prove that accounts rendered *without* any other enclosure are more likely to receive immediate attention, but an occasional exception is very worth while.

The value of personal contacts is not to be overlooked. Booksellers must literally 'go out for business'; it will not all just come to the shop. Regular courtesy-calls on local librarians, schoolmasters, and secretaries of clubs and institutions will build up friendship and goodwill, and inevitably bring more business in the course of time. Above all the shop must always have the owner, manager or senior sales assistant on the shop floor ready to receive customers and give expert personal attention. This is often neglected because there are so many publishers' representatives regularly calling, but they must never be allowed to detract from the service to the customers.

Finally, in all displays, publicity and sales promotion the golden rule is 'watch your competitors and watch other trades'; there is always something to learn. Be quick to use new ideas and new methods of approach. The booksellers' task is to bring books to the notice of the public. Do not be discouraged by a few failures, as these are inevitable from time to time, but doubtless there will be more successes to record—sometimes from some simple feature on which little store was originally set. Time after time a signing session by an author which one feared might be a 'flop' proves to be an outstanding success. The lesson to be learned is that it is a mistake not to try.

Booksellers' Catalogues

The possibility of obtaining extra sales by sending out catalogues is well known to booksellers, and even small booksellers find that it pays to issue them. From records kept over several years it has been proved that many catalogues pay directly; and it must be remembered that it is not possible to trace all orders, as only a percentage of personal shoppers are likely to mention that they have come to buy a book because they have seen it in a catalogue. Even when a catalogue does not pay directly, it is usually a fairly cheap advertisement if care is exercised in keeping the cost of production within reasonable limits. Elaborate catalogues are issued by firms which can afford them, but inexpensive catalogues and lists—even duplicated lists—can be issued and used with good effect by smaller bookshops.

There is a tendency for catalogues of books to follow a pattern, and this may be a mistake. It is wise to aim at producing a catalogue that is in some respects different from the usual type. Another tendency is for catalogues to be too long. It has been proved that two catalogues of, say, eight pages will almost certainly bring more business than one catalogue of sixteen pages. There is, of course, the expense of two postings but, on the other hand, customers are reminded twice of the bookseller's business and, if the first catalogue arrived at an inopportune moment, the second may be more fortunate; if a customer is offered too much at once in a long catalogue, he may be bewildered.

It is possible for almost any bookseller to issue a well-illustrated catalogue at no great expense if he will borrow suitable blocks from the publishers, who will be found most co-operative in this way. A catalogue should be attractive not only in appearance but in its compilation. It should reflect the particular nature of the business. Cataloguing is an art; a great deal must be learned by trial and error, but much knowledge can be acquired by studying other firms' catalogues.

Plan the Catalogue

It is advisable to begin the compilation of a catalogue by drawing up a plan of work. It will almost certainly be found difficult to keep to that plan, but it is well to have the shape and form mapped out at the start. If it is desired to produce an eight-page Christmas list, for instance, the first thing to decide is the size, and then to place together sheets of paper of that size. It is necessary to decide whether or not illustrations are going to be used, and of which kind, as on that decision will depend the type and size of the paper that is ordered. The next step is to arrange roughly the headings which are to be used and the pages on which they are to appear. It may be decided to have two or more columns on each. Make a rough plan of the catalogue on the eight pages of plain paper, starting off on the first page with an outline of the front cover and putting the name and address of the bookseller at the foot of every page. It will be necessary to have some idea of the type proposed, as this will govern the amount of 'copy' required for each page. Specimens of type sizes and faces can be obtained from printers, or a catalogue of another firm may be used as a guide to the printer on the general style required. You should not, of course, copy blindly the other firm's layout. With the aid of these specimens, the bookseller should work out roughly the number of items that can be catalogued on each column or page. All is then ready for starting the actual cataloguing of the books on plain index cards or sheets of paper. The selection of books is obviously all-important, and no less important is the way in which they are described. When cataloguing each item it is a good plan to classify it and write the classification on the back of the card or elsewhere in such a way that the compositor will understand that it is not to be set up in type.

The reason why it is desirable to classify at the time of cataloguing is to avoid error. Titles can be misleading, and a book may subsequently be included in the wrong section unless every precaution is taken. Wide classifications, like sport and travel, biography, books for the home, or reference books, are often to be preferred to narrower classifications.

When cards or slips of paper have been prepared in sufficient number to fill the catalogue they are sorted; and it will almost certainly be found that some adjustments have to be made because of there being too many items in some classifications and too few in others. This obviously entails either alteration of the original plan or the writing of more cards for short sections, if matter can be found to fit into them, and the deletion of items from those sections that are too long. At one time it was usual to catalogue in the order of author, initials, title, sub-title, size, date and price, but today a catalogue of new books can be presented much more attractively to the public. It is not possible to give hard-and-fast rules, but the title, followed by the name of the author, a brief description and the price is an effective catalogue order for some booksellers. The arrangement depends very much on the type of catalogue, and much will be learned from a study of the arrangement of other catalogues and lists. When illustrations are to be used, the position of these must be indicated in the rough plan which accompanies the 'copy' when it is sent to the printer. Many printers will set up type from cards or slips but when the bookseller has a typist he should have the matter typed first. Printers' errors due to bad handwriting will thus be minimized.

Proof-reading

When the printer's proofs are received, they must be corrected with the 'copy' and to do this properly it is advisable to check two or three times. It is quite a good plan to read the proofs the first time without reference to the copy, as in this way it will more likely be noticed where a change of word or alteration of style is desirable; the second check with the copy should be for accuracy of spelling, prices and other details. Prices should be given particular attention. It is always wise to get a second person to read a proof because, however careful one may be, errors *can* slip through, so another person's assistance is always advisable. Do not omit to check every page heading, name and address, and telephone number. There are often mistakes in these, showing that the checker has concentrated on the books listed and forgotten the rest.

When the proofs arrive it is also good practice to take the

opportunity of checking the stock to see that the books listed are adequately represented. If not, they must either be reordered for stock or deleted from the catalogue. Nothing is more annoying and damaging to a bookseller than to issue a list and fail to produce the books when they are ordered.

To return to the correction of the proofs, this is a simple matter which can be undertaken without special knowledge of proof correction. If a wrong letter is used, simply put a line through it and write the correct one in the margin. If a word or part of a word is to be omitted, put a line through it and write 'delete' in the margin. If the position of a word or part of a word is to be altered, encircle it and with a line indicate its position, writing 'transpose' in the margin. It is nevertheless strongly recommended that some knowledge of printers' correction marks and the way to correct proofs be acquired. This is not difficult; full particulars are given in *Rules for Compositors and Readers*, by Horace Hart (Oxford University Press). They appear also in many other reference books, including *Pears Cyclopaedia* and Sir Stanley Unwin's *The Truth about Publishing*.

When the proof is corrected and returned to the printer it is as well to confirm the number of copies required. (Estimates and samples of paper will, of course, have been obtained previously and an order placed.) The cost of setting up is the heaviest item, and it does not cost very much more to have one or two thousand extra copies run off when once the type is set.

The dispatching of the catalogues should not be done in a haphazard manner. They must be posted at the psychological moment. I advise spreading postings over a week or two as this automatically means some spread of the orders received which helps the mail-order section, but more importantly it safeguards against some of those disasters which can minimize business such as strikes, bad news on the Stock Exchange or severe weather making shopping difficult. It is usually a great advantage to arrange, as far as possible, for catalogues to be posted on a day which will ensure their being delivered in time for reading at the week-end, and preferably at the end of the month, as many salaries are paid at that time.

If a record of sales resulting from the issue of the catalogue is required, it can be made quite simply by marking a copy, or one or two copies pasted in a book, or better still in two books, one for the order room and one for the shop. Simply mark the figure 1 by the title for each sale, and total these when the catalogue has been issued some time and sales resulting from it have practically ceased. If many of one title are sold, the gate system of marking can be used, thus ̶I̶I̶I̶I, which equals 5. This makes addition easy; ̶I̶I̶I̶I ̶I̶I̶I̶I 11 = 12 sold.

Catalogues and prospectuses should always contain order forms. These can be printed as part of the catalogue or prospectus. To make ordering simple for the customer, some firms number each item listed so that the customer need give only the number and title instead of full details. This practice is particularly useful in a catalogue of antiquarian or second-hand books.

Coloured inks, coloured papers, ornamental borders and lettering all have their place in catalogue production, but it is advisable to use them sparingly. A bookseller's catalogue should always be in good taste.

10

Mail Orders

Mail-order bookselling presents many challenges but there is enormous scope for selling books by mail order to people residing both in this country and abroad. It is often claimed that selling through the post is not a very profitable form of bookselling because of the heavy labour costs and overheads, and this is often true. Of course, in many businesses it is quite possible for someone to deal with a few mail orders in between serving customers in the shop, and this is profitable. It usually takes a long time to build up a large postal trade, which is done by advertisement and the sending of catalogues and lists. Good mail-order bookselling is as much an art as selling in the shop itself; there are the same opportunities for suggestion selling, for recording the particular subjects in which customers are interested, and for maintaining goodwill by courteous and above all speedy attention. Speed and accuracy are the essentials in all mail-order selling.

The amount of time taken in dealing with even a relatively small mail-order trade is quite considerable, and if not carefully controlled can be so unprofitable as to be more of a drain on the business than an asset. With sound control it can become a very valuable asset indeed.

Customers rarely understand the complexities of the business and cause endless trouble by not knowing how to order. If only all could write clearly, particularly their names and addresses, and give all the necessary information about the books they require, the task of mail-order bookselling would be easier. It can never be simple, however, because customers cannot be expected to know the names of the publishers of all the books they want, and many out-of-the-way books and pamphlets are ordered through the post, often doubtless because the customer has failed to obtain them from the local bookseller.

However difficult customers may make the lot of the bookseller, it is of primary importance in mail-order bookselling that things are made as easy as possible for the customer. For instance, a supply of order forms, one with each out-going parcel, will be found to be very helpful. The cost is quickly recovered by the obtaining of more orders and the saving in labour costs, as printed order forms simplify matters in a variety of ways. Customers may make every conceivable error when ordering. They may give the heading of a review instead of the title of the book. They may order a book they have 'seen in your window' and of which they 'unfortunately' have forgotten the title. A description follows, and after careful search and further correspondence the bookseller may discover that it was not in his window that the book was seen, but in that of some other bookshop, possibly in another town. Many examples of customers' errors could be given. The customers, however, are not always wrong, but when they are tact is necessary in pointing out their errors in such a way as not to lose future custom.

Mail-order Routine

Mail-order routine varies according to the size and nature of the business. A system is here outlined which has been used over many years by competent booksellers with a good postal trade supported by a good shop trade.

Orders through the post must be opened by a person in a responsible position, as some will include money in one form or another, such as cheques, postal orders, or book tokens. When the letters are opened they should be date-stamped and all enclosures noted at the top of the actual letter—for example, cheque £5.25, book token £1.00, and it is advisable to note the actual numbers of the Treasury notes or tokens, or at least the last two figures. Complaints must be dealt with immediately and urgent orders put in hand at once. In my early days in bookselling all letters had to be numbered and entered in a letter-book. The surname, initials, address and total of money enclosed were registered, but where there is a large mail-order business this system is obsolete. Of course, any money sent with mail orders must go straight to the counting-house or cashier. Although letters and orders are in many businesses no longer recorded they are often numbered and there exists a small machine not much larger than a rubber stamp dating machine which does this, the number changing automatically. For filing for easy reference, orders are best filed alphabetically. The alphabet may be divided into all the letters of the alphabet, if the size of the business requires it, or into two, A–K and L–Z, or into four, A–D, E–K, L–R and S–Z.

When the orders are properly dated and numbered they are passed to assistants to look out from stock the books ordered and to write on the letter the replies to any inquiries. In the case of a lengthy reply, it may be necessary to pin to the letter an extra piece of paper on which details have been given.

If all the books ordered were always in stock, mail-order bookselling would, of course, be simple and speedy, but unfortunately this can rarely be the case. When an order cannot be completed at once the assistant may adopt one of two courses. He may send off immediately the books in stock and later those obtained a few days or weeks after and record the other books temporarily unobtainable in such a way as to ensure that the customer will be sent the books or notified at once when the books are available. The second course is to send an acknowledgement in response to orders where there is to be delay in supplying, and to send the complete consignment of books when all are to hand. The only advantage in the second course is that the customer is possibly saved some postage, but the disadvantage is that he does not receive any books immediately. Again in past years when postage and time were inexpensive all orders were acknowledged but that is unnecessary unless it is known that there will be long delay. In no circumstances should part of the order be dispatched without explanation, *with the consignment*, of why the other books were not included. If this is not done the customer will write to complain or inquire about the books which he has not received and this increases costly correspondence.

Before books are dispatched they must, unless the correct money accompanies the order, be charged to the account of the customer. This necessitates recording the name and address of the customer, titles and prices of the books supplied, cost of the postage and packing and the total amount due. On dispatch an invoice (or a receipt, where payment accompanies the order) is enclosed in the parcel, and correct records are sent to the accounts department. *Invoices, letters, etc., must never be inserted in books in such a way that they can be overlooked; they should be folded round the face of the jacket of the top book in the parcel and partly inserted in the front cover*, or enclosed in an envelope the flap of which only is inserted in the top book of the parcel.

The orders which have been completely dealt with are filed in either numerical or alphabetical order. Alphabetical order is, in my view, generally more satisfactory.

The completion of orders received by post is one of the chief difficulties of mail-order bookselling. It should be possible to devise a foolproof system which records those books required by customers that are temporarily unobtainable, and which ensures that they are supplied as soon as stocks are again available. This can be achieved where the system is computerized but it is difficult otherwise. Some booksellers use a book with numbered pages preceded by an alphabetical thumb-index. The titles are entered in the index and a page, or part of a page, is given to each title in the body of the record. For instance, orders received for *Churchill Memoirs* would probably take up several pages, so the thumb-index would, under *C*, record '*Churchill Memoirs*', 100–6. Pages 100–6 in the book would be headed '*Churchill Memoirs*' and on them the names and addresses from the letters ordering the book would be recorded. The weakness of this system is its reliance on the human element for the degree of accuracy, prompt dispatch, and completion of orders. It is easy, in the case of an important book like that of Sir Winston, to complete orders promptly, but many orders are placed for books which are not so easily remembered, and it is possible for such books to find their way into stock instead of being correctly connected with the customer's order. Obviously this will lead to a complaint, as the customer may see the book in another book-seller's shop or in some other way will know sooner or later that the title is again available. A regular weekly check by a first-class assistant seeing all the fresh stock before it goes on to the shelves minimizes the risk, but some books will almost certainly still be overlooked.

A separate file of incomplete orders is necessary. Orders, as previously stated, are filed away on completion, under either name or number, but 'incomplete' orders are best kept under the customer's name in a separate file after they have been entered in an awaiting-completion book. It is, of course, important to mark clearly the items in the book when they are supplied. It is an advantage also to record the number of the invoice, date of dispatch, and other particulars such as 'Call Order' (an order for books to be called for by the customer).

A high standard of letter-writing should be aimed at when corresponding with customers as it is expected of booksellers. It is well to avoid the use of trade terms as far as possible. Even those that are now almost in general use, such as 'Out of Print' and 'Reprinting', are apt to be used loosely and may cause misunderstanding. Where it is possible to convey an accurate meaning in non-technical language it is always to be preferred. Experience shows that the term 'Out of Print' is often used in error for 'Reprinting'. As I have said earlier, 'Reprinting' can convey the idea to the customer that copies will shortly be available again, whereas months and sometimes years may elapse before supplies arrive.

It is common practice to write 'A' and the date, or 'Ack' and the date, at the top of the customer's letter in order to indicate acknowledgement, and to affix the carbon copy of the letter of reply, or to note against the titles such explanatory terms as 'Reprinting' or 'Binding' and to tick them (and perhaps give the date), to indicate that this explanation has been given to the

customer. It is also usual to tick or cross off on the letter the titles
of the books as they are looked out.

Postage and Packing Charges

As the cost of servicing mail orders is costly in time, stationery,
etc., a bookseller must charge the customer enough to cover the
cost, not only of postage, but of packing material and time.
Weigh the book or books, allow about 1 lb for the weight of the
wrapping material, ascertain the postage and add on about half
that amount. Example: a book weighs 1½ lb, packing material
brings it up to 2½ lb, postage abroad is, say, 30p; charge to the
customer 45p.[1]

In mail-order bookselling it is necessary to read carefully the
letters received. This may sound superfluous advice, but it is
surprising how many mistakes are made because the assistant
failed to read the letter properly. For instance, he may note the
name at the foot of the letter and the address at the top, and send
the books to that name and address, whereas instructions may be
embodied in the letter to send the books to some other person at a
different address. It is also advisable to copy the name and address
from the letter on to the invoice, and from the invoice to the label;
then if the information on the label agrees with that in the letter
it follows that the address must be correct on all entries.

Pro forma invoices are sent when payment *in advance* is required.
An invoice headed *Pro Forma*, giving particulars of the books,
prices, postage and the total amount required, is sent to the
customer, possibly with an accompanying letter.

Mail-order assistants could very often substantially increase the
business by suggesting alternatives when the actual books required
are not available, or even by substitution (returnable), particularly
at Christmas time. I recommend every bookseller to try this
substitution say during the last posting at Christmas. Some
customers will complain but most will think your service and
thoughtfulness are marvellous! Booksellers usually receive their

[1] In the United Kingdom VAT is chargeable on postage and packing when
the charges for these are shown on an invoice as a separate item.

largest number of orders through the post at the Christmas season and, as the books are, of course, frequently required for gifts, the customers generally welcome suggestions, particularly in the case of children's books, if the books ordered are not available. When books are substituted a letter of explanation must accompany them, and it is suggested that booksellers would do extra business if they had duplicated or printed in advance a letter something along these lines:

> We have taken the liberty of substituting .... for titles ordered, because we are out of stock of the latter. To avoid delay and as Christmas is so near, we felt you would prefer these books rather than wait until after Christmas for the titles you ordered. Should we have failed, however, to meet your wishes and requirements, the book(s) sent may be returned within seven days.

A surprising amount of extra business has resulted when I have substituted, but only if done a few days before Christmas and for children's books, and in the main goodwill was enhanced.

A Classified List of Customers' Interests

The keeping of a list of customers and the types of books in which they are interested is possibly the most neglected sales potential in bookselling. The value of an index of customers, classified under subjects, cannot be overestimated. The compilation is a simple matter, but keen assistants are the only people who can build up such a record and keep it up to date.

In a slack period it is possible to scrutinize all mail orders received during the busy periods, and to make a classified index in accordance with the titles ordered. But in most shops the opportunities of increasing sales by following up the particular interests of customers who buy in the shop are often partly or wholly lost because sales assistants have not sufficient time or industry to compile an index. It is easier, perhaps, in large book-shops where certain assistants are in charge of separate sections, such as art, nature, music, theatre, ballet, etc., for an index to be compiled, as the assistant will have a special interest in the development of his section, and will watch sales and draw up as large a mailing list as possible ready for the prospectuses and catalogues likely to appeal to his customers. In a business where the sales are general and assistants do not specialize, it is difficult to get them to compile a good classified index, more especially in busy shops where assistants can fill in all their time serving and arranging stock. Nevertheless, with extra effort and keenness it can usually be done. A list of buyers of books on angling, golf, horse-racing, biography, travel and photography, to mention but a few subjects, is invaluable, particularly when an important book is to be published and a good prospectus is available in advance.

There is a complication in compiling a classified index, owing to the fact that many people are interested in a variety of subjects. A keen golfer may also be interested in ballet, and he may have children, so there are three classifications; golf, ballet and children's books. But broader classifications will be found more useful; for example, instead of golf—sport; instead of ballet—the stage.

In a case such as I have instanced, it would be necessary to make out three index cards for the customer and file one under each subject. This is laborious and expensive, and it must be remembered that many book-buyers are interested in a dozen or so subjects. Several ways of overcoming this difficulty suggest themselves, but one which will appeal to small businesses is the use of an indexed book instead of cards. In a book can be recorded the names of the customers in alphabetical order, the addresses, and the subjects in which they are interested. If the list is not long, it is not difficult to go through it and count the number of customers interested in, say, golf, and order prospectuses accordingly, or to address envelopes from the list to all customers interested in children's books or any other of the recorded classifications. Another method is to have a 'general' section in which are filed cards of those customers with such wide interests that they are worth circularizing with almost every available list or prospectus. On this 'general' index card special subjects known to be those of particular interest can be mentioned. Before an index is compiled it is advisable to make a list of necessary classifications; this may be altered from time to time. If wider classifications are used, more exact information can be recorded on the cards.

'Weeding' Mailing Lists

While the success of mail-order bookselling depends to no small extent on making the *process of ordering books* easy for the customer, it is possible to make the ordering of *lists* of books on special subjects too easy. For instance, there are issued by publishers and booksellers from time to time request slips or letters containing a list of subjects with a heading, 'please tick those in which you are interested'. Customers are usually generous with the 'ticks' and in consequence the bookseller is put to much expense in sending lists to customers who may be slightly interested in the majority of the subjects.

Constant attention should be given to mailing lists so that they are kept up to date and unnecessary expense avoided. Not only must the name and address be kept up to date, but purchases should be recorded so that the names of those customers who do not order within a specified period can be removed. This, however, must be done with care, as important contacts can be lost by the removal of the names of customers who may place good orders at very long intervals.

To assist in the 'weeding out' of a mailing list it is suggested that at long intervals a reply-paid postcard be enclosed with a catalogue or list with a request for its completion if catalogues are still required. A short note on the following lines would meet the case:

> Dear Sir
>
> We have had the pleasure of sending you catalogues, and we hope you have found them useful. We are revising our mailing lists and, if you would like to have further catalogues, kindly complete this postcard.

You will probably be surprised to find that very few of the cards are returned, and your catalogue list is consequently substantially reduced. Some of the customers may subsequently ask why they are no longer receiving catalogues, but when it is explained to them that before the mailing lists were revised they were notified they will be found to be quite reasonable.

There are many valuable references from which names and addresses of potential book buyers can be obtained, such as *Who's Who*, telephone directories, electoral rolls, etc. When a specialized list is issued, valuable names and addresses can frequently be obtained from the secretary of a society of members interested in that particular subject. If he is not co-operative you may know a customer who belongs to such a society, who may be helpful in lending you a list of members. Secretaries of societies will usually be found helpful if it is explained to them that the names and address are required so that a valuable list of books which will specially appeal to members may be sent to them. The straightforward approach, and in particular a personal call, is strongly recommended, and (who knows) you may make another customer or a lifelong friend, or both.

Opportunities to sell, to make extra sales, occur every hour of the day, but many are lost by lack of knowledge and more often by lack of sufficient interest and understanding of the customer's requirements. How many booksellers include a prospectus or two in every parcel taken or posted? It is amazing what extra sales result from making it a practice that every posted or delivered parcel contains up to three prospectuses and every book placed in a bag in the shop by the assistant is accompanied by at least one prospectus. It is a good practice for sales assistants to place prospectuses in the bags first thing every morning ready for the busy period, otherwise in the rush this most valuable sales promotion may be lost. Small prospectuses, catalogues or lists can be included with correspondence to advantage.

11

Cash and Credit Sales and Stock Control

The main volume of business in most bookshops is on cash sales basis, and in these days most shops have cash registers. There are many types of cash register, including one-drawer to four-drawer machines, and registers are available to record sales by department or by each assistant, and even to calculate change.

In many bookshops several assistants use the same cash register with one drawer, in others, each assistant has a separate cash register or a drawer in one. The advantage of each assistant having a separate register helps ensure accurate recording of transactions and tends to minimize theft by staff. The four-drawer or even the two-drawer register in a busy shop has the disadvantage that frequently more than one assistant is struggling to ring up the transaction, put the money in the drawer and get change at the same time.

In the old days bookshops had a cash desk near the entrance staffed by a cashier and in shops of a certain size this is still a system which has many advantages. If cashiers are employed in cash desks, other duties can also be allotted to them, such as the giving of information regarding the whereabouts of certain sections of books, and the sale of book tokens, and at slack times there are other useful jobs which can be undertaken. There is no doubt that the presence of an alert cashier minimizes the theft of books, particularly if the cash desk is near the exit, as potential thieves can never be sure whether or not their actions are being watched from the cash desk.

When a cash desk with a cashier is used, stealing by staff is also minimized, particularly if the customers may only pay at the cash desk, and sales assistants are not permitted to take money. The system is simple; assistants are required to enter titles in their cash books with the total of purchase, retaining the carbon copy. They tear out the top docket, which is perforated in the middle so that it will tear easily into two parts, and this is handed to the customer to take to the cask desk to make payment. The cashier retains one part and the customer returns to the sales assistant with the other half, which has been stamped by the cashier to show the customer has paid. Books can be wrapped by the assistant while the customer goes to the cash desk. If it is made a strict rule that assistants may on no account handle money, regular breach of the rule would soon be noticed and the matter investigated.

The assistants must be instructed never to allow customers to take books before they have been paid for at the cash desk—unless debited to account—because this inevitably leads to a few customers walking out with books, together with the cash docket, without paying.

In my experience many assistants find it difficult to give accurate change consistently, doubtless because their heads are filled with book titles and their minds are grappling with questions concerning books about which customers inquire while the assistants are working out the change; any system which leaves the giving of change to a cashier is best, but in large busy shops this is often impracticable as customers cannot be expected to fight their way through a mass of shoppers and browsers to pay for the books they want and fight their way back with the receipted docket to pick up the parcel from the sales assistant. However desirable cash desks may be they are disappearing and cash registers with their limitations are taking their place.

Whatever system is used for taking and recording cash, some method of recording the titles sold is also necessary to ensure the prompt reordering of books required for stock. But this in itself is not enough to maintain sound stocks, because the stock which has to be ordered is not only that which is sold, but includes titles asked for which are not in stock. In large businesses a book may

be asked for say six or more times from different assistants, and
the buyer must have some means of knowing this. It is, therefore,
a sound policy to give each assistant a special book for entering
the following details:

(a) Titles of all books asked for but not in stock.
(b) Titles which are selling out quickly.

In this book it is well to encourage the writing of suggestions of
all kinds regarding stock. Remarks from assistants such as 'No
books on horse-riding', 'We are often asked for maps of France',
'We are short of phrase books for travellers going to the Continent', are most valuable. This works well generally, but tends to
break down in busy seasons, as assistants simply have not the
time to make the necessary entries.

Stock Control

Stock control obviously must be linked with sales so various
systems are devised to enable the buyers to reorder books to
replace sold stock. I have never found a system that is wholly
satisfactory and some can be dangerous inasmuch as they can lead
to rather automatic replacement of stock, resulting in over-
buying.

Books cannot be automatically reordered for stock, as can tins
of sardines or packets of soap-flakes. There comes a time when the
bookseller breathes a sigh of relief when the last copy of a title is
sold and the last thing he wants is for it to be reordered. Stock
control can be useful nevertheless in certain sections such as
Paperbacks or Children's Books and is particularly useful in
specialist bookshops where the same titles sell over a period of
years.

One simple system has been used by the trade over many
years but before explaining it I should state that booksellers
should avoid systems which entail overmuch detail work.
Obviously if a card is to be prepared for every title in stock as in
the system outlined below, it will be costly in time and material.

The Order-Card System

This is a system designed to maintain adequate replacement of stock, and minimize loss of sales. When stock arrives from the publisher an ordinary index card is prepared on which is entered author, title, price, number of copies purchased and the date the stock was received. The bottom half-inch of the card (folded to ensure its protruding from the book) is reserved for the name of the author and the title. The other particulars can be recorded at the top of the card, and subsequent purchases and sales entered thereon from time to time.

The card is placed in one copy of the title to which it refers, and when the last copy is sold it is removed and placed in a box and these cards are collected daily to be examined by the buyer for reordering purposes. In my experience this is not a very good system. It falls down in several ways. First, new stock can be held up awaiting the writing of index cards and sales are lost. Secondly, the card is often 'sold' with the book and the system breaks down. In a small shop a good bookseller will 'know' his stock and no card system is necessary. In a large shop the poor buyer would, with the above system, have hundreds of cards to scrutinize daily. Nevertheless the system or something rather similar is used successfully, particularly where publishers' representatives pay infrequent visits.

A rather simpler system which will be found useful in a shop of any size with a wide range of stock, particularly in a shop which is split up into departments yet controlled by a single buyer, is to make out a simple record card detailing:

Author, title, price, publisher.
Number ordered with order number and date.
Date received.
Any reports, e.g. binding.
The reorder level for that title.

The card is often made out when the buyer subscribes the title from a representative and the quantity subscribed is indicated on the card or subsequently by a clerk working from the buyer's order book. Thereafter all stock orders are noted on it, and over a number of months a pattern of sales can be established, and often for standard works a reorder level can be worked out and noted. The system is designed primarily to avoid sales being lost through being out of a title.

The cards should be kept in separate boxes or filing cabinets and each assistant can have a section to look after and check. This gives him an interest in the running of the business, although the actual reordering of stock may still be done by the buyer. More important still, because all information about the title is written down on the card, any assistant, no matter how new or inexperienced, is in a position to consult the card and give information to customers. The reorder level and regular checking ensures that important titles are always in stock, but if from the card it is seen that the title is selling very slowly, the card can be marked in some way so that the title is not reordered when the last copy is sold.

A stock-control card system consists of the record and the reminder, which can be combined on one card, as suggested above. Such a system gives an accurate history of the sale of each book, and does not rely on the infallibility of the buyer's memory. The system should always be an aid to buying; the bookseller must run the system, not the system run the bookseller.

Having dealt with simple systems of stock control I return to Sales. Orders will be taken for books which are not in stock, and it is important that the assistant takes the name and address of the customer, even if the customer says he will call for the book. Where possible, it is advisable to obtain on the actual order the signature of the customer. When books are ordered there is always a risk that the customer will not return for them. Some booksellers obtain a deposit as a safeguard, particularly if the books ordered are not in general demand. Booksellers can lose considerably by obtaining books to order if customers do not return and buy them. By obtaining a signature this risk seems to be minimized, but a still better way is to have a special book of order-slips printed in the form of a contract to buy, with a duplicate for the customer to take away with him as a reminder.

If books are obtained to order and are not collected in, say a week, a postcard should be sent to the customer, notifying him that the book is awaiting collection.[1] In the event of any books ordered not being obtainable, the customer should be notified through the post if he does not call in for the information.

Orders for popular general books may usually be safely taken without a deposit, but orders for very expensive or specialized books, such as legal or technical and medical books, should not be accepted from unknown customers without a deposit or some measure of certainty that the customers will return and definitely buy the books. If the bookseller is 'caught' with an expensive book because the customer ordering it did not return, the publisher will often oblige by accepting its return for credit if he is asked promptly and told the facts. If the 'call shelf' is neglected, and in my experience this is all too often the case, a bookseller can lose a lot of money. It is most important that someone be made responsible for it to ensure that customers are informed and, where necessary, reminded that the book they ordered awaits collection, and after a reasonable time uncalled-for books must go into stock or, if likely to be unsaleable, returned, by arrangement, to the publisher.

Computers

It has become the practice in recent years for larger bookshops or groups to computerize their records and accounts. This does not necessarily entail the purchase of a computer, as there are in existence Computer Bureaux specializing in processing work for the smaller businesses. The service they provide can cover administrative records, such as orders, Bought and Sales ledger accounts, etc. Most bureaux can provide a service in three different ways:

---

[1] Suggested wording for postcard:

We are pleased to inform you that we have obtained ....
and will keep it in reserve for seven days.

If you would like us to post it kindly return this Card with a remittance (including postage).

Price................................   Postage................................

(a) Punching and Coding information such as Invoices, Charges to Customers' Accounts, etc., supplied by the bookseller and renting time at the bureau.
(b) Bureau punching and processing the information as indicated above, but leaving controlling and checking of work to the bookseller.
(c) Bureau can do the complete job including Bought and Sales ledgers accounts punching, processing and checking information.

If Schemes (a) or (b) were adopted the bookseller would be faced with the cost of programming, which is expensive. By adopting Scheme (c) a nominal fee is paid to the bureau for use of a standard package. Whatever scheme is adopted there are, of course, computer running costs and cost of stationery, and if Scheme (a) were adopted there would also be the cost of the punching machines.

By the use of computers for controlling work, the following can be provided. For a Bought Ledger System, a bookseller could receive:

Remittance advice to customer.
Copy remittance advice for ledger records.
Cheque made out to suppliers (only signature required).
Cash payments book.
Analysis of purchases and expenses.
Name and address records of suppliers' accounts.
Suppliers' cumulative records of purchases to date.

For a Sales Ledger System a bookseller would receive each month the following:

Validation Report.
Update Report.
Customer balances outstanding.
Mailing labels.
Customer record cards.
Department Sales Analysis.
Invoices.

Statements.
Work in progress report.
Stock value analysis.
Overdue letters.
Name and address update report.
Transactions update report.
Customer balances current.

In conclusion the use of computers should result in:

Records being kept more efficiently.
Some reduction in staff and thereby savings in salaries and wages. Business can expand without extra office staff.
Saving as there is no longer need to employ machine operators, invoice typists, etc.
Eliminating the cost of accounting and ancillary machines.
Remittance advices, statements and accounting records always on time.

❧❧❧❧❧❧❧❧❧❧❧❧❧❧❧❧❧❧❧❧❧❧❧❧❧❧❧❧❧❧❧❧❧

12

Stock and Stocktaking

In most bookshops, the stock on the shelves and that displayed on the tables is only a part of the total stock. Because of limitations of ground-floor shelving space, or indeed of total shelving space, it is usually necessary to have a stockroom and to keep parcels of books in the basement, or sometimes under or on the top of fixtures. Therefore some system of replacing stock sold from the shelves by drawing on these reserves is obviously necessary.

In many bookshops stock reserves kept in parcels or in cup-boards are apt to be forgotten—'out of sight out of mind'—and the system must not rely too much on the memory of staff or sales will be constantly lost and books already in stock reordered. The fact that these books may well be slow-sellers does not improve matters.

First, then, any system of stock-keeping which does away with storing books in brown-paper parcels is to be recommended. If parcels cannot be avoided, the recording and labelling of their contents must be given careful and constant attention. The advantage of parcelling books is primarily that it keeps them clean, but the disadvantages can outweigh the advantages, as parcelling also keeps them out of sight. Not only are some sales lost but the opportunity of returning books or of claiming when they are remaindered, or when a cheap or new edition or revised edition is published, may also be missed. In some bookshops any parcelled stock is card-indexed. The card index is, however, frequently found to have been misused or neglected and to be no longer accurate. Again, parcels are frequently burst open by assistants who wish to obtain a book quickly, and the label may be so torn that the contents are not easily identified.

If a bookseller is fortunate enough to have good stock shelves or cupboards it is best to leave the stock unwrapped, and to place the books on a sheet of paper on each shelf, and have them dusted regularly. The stocks of books in stockrooms, etc., can best be kept 'under observation' by having a 'Key' shelf, which is made up of one copy of each book of which there are reserve stocks. This key shelf is in every way superior to any card-index. Its advantage is that booksellers (usually possessing a photographic eye) are, by frequent glances at the key shelf, reminded of the titles of the stock stored away. Frequent reference to a card-index does not assist the mind to the same degree. Secondly, the keeping of the key shelf entails no writing of index cards; a simple reference number, giving the number of the shelf or fixture where the stock is placed, should be lightly pencilled on the jacket at the foot of the spine of each book on the Key shelf.

This key shelf of books should not be in a position in the shop where customers are able to withdraw books from it but should be in an office, staff room or recess not frequented by customers. Large businesses could use two key shelves—one in the mail-order room for the use of the staff engaged on post work, and another in a small recess of the book department for the use of staff engaged in selling to personal shoppers and for those responsible for bringing forward new stock to the shop as sales are made. Another advantage of this system is that, if by some chance the reserve stock is exhausted, the customer is not disappointed, as the last copy—the key copy itself—can then be sold. The possible danger of the system breaking down by the removal of key copies when stocks are held can be overcome by monthly checks against stock. This necessitates only collecting a copy of each of the reserves, checking it with the key shelf and then replacing it if not wanted there. Before replacing, it is well to make sure that at least one copy is on the shelves in the shop in its correct classification as it may be that copies have been sold from the shelves and fresh copies not brought forward.

Reserve stocks may be arranged under the names of the publishers or authors for easy reference. A smooth-working arrangement is to keep stocks under publishers and the key shelf under authors, but the deciding factors are size of reserve stocks, space available and, particularly, the kind of space available.

All shelves or fixtures in bookshops should, of course, be numbered. This is vital for stocktaking and useful in a variety of ways. For this purpose, small stick-on numbered labels can be purchased cheaply and affixed at the top of the side-strip of the shelf in a position where the label will not be rubbed off and where the number can easily be seen even when the shelf is full of books, but not presenting an unsightly appearance. There are neater methods of achieving this, and neatness is important, so keep on the look-out for economic and tasteful methods of numbering and of shelf classification systems.

Stocktaking

The main purpose of stocktaking is to ascertain as near as possible the true value of the total stock, and in bookselling this is not easy. For instance, at stocktaking it is of primary importance to make certain that all invoices and credit notes are put through in their correct financial year, otherwise, however carefully one has assessed the value of the stock on the shelves the total figure for the financial year will be incorrect. It is difficult in bookselling to ensure that all invoices and credits are correctly recorded, because many consignments of books arrive without invoices, so if due care is not exercised books can be sold or taken from stock and invoices for them passed in the next financial year instead of in the year to which they apply.

To make this point clear, supposing in the week or so before Christmas books arrive without invoices and are either sold or taken into stock on the shelves; at stocktaking early in the New Year the stock figure will be too high by the total of such sales or stock unless a note has been made of the total of invoices outstanding. When the invoices ultimately arrive they must be entered in the books correctly. Publishers are notoriously slow in sending credits so supposing books have been returned for credit, say to a total value of £500, this 'asset' must be added to the stock for stocktaking purposes, but when the credits arrive they must appear in the financial records in such a way that the value is not added to the stock figure again or in the wrong financial year.

There are several methods of stocktaking and all are designed to achieve the same result, i.e. to ascertain the true value of the stock (not necessarily the cost), but some methods have become antiquated and cumbersome. In these days any unnecessary paper-work or elaboration of system is costly in time and money, so the simplest way which ensures the required degree of accuracy is the best. Some firms take days or even weeks stocktaking but in Hatchards we can accurately ascertain the value of all books in stock in a few hours. We close the shop for stocktaking and the staff start work promptly at 9 a.m. Usually the staff are free to go home soon after lunchtime as their work is done.

The simplest and best system I know *for General Bookselling* is the one used at Hatchards. It is as follows:

1. Arrange in advance to hire a number of adding machines.
2. The day before stocktaking fix to the top of each tier of shelves a large envelope bearing a number.
3. Divide the staff up into pairs. One person to call out (not so loudly as to disturb the others) and one to record on an adding machine.
4. Staff must be instructed to provide *one* slip from the adding machine detailing the prices of all books in the tier and *one total for each tier*. They are required to enter at the top of each slip the number of the tier plus the classification, thus

> 6
> FICTION

One total is similarly required for each table display, free-standing units and for each window, or office. It is important that staff understand that they must total each tier and not run on from one tier to the next.

5. The adding-machine slips are left in the fixtures tucked between

books but protruding so they can be gathered up, one slip in each tier.

6. All slips are gathered up by the Manager or Accounts Manager who takes them away to arrive at a grand total. It is possible for him not only to obtain the grand total of stock but to obtain totals for various classifications, which is useful information for stock control.

7. Having obtained the Grand Total at Selling Price of all stock, it is reduced to approximate cost by deducting 40 per cent or 33⅓ per cent plus. The plus, of say 10 per cent, will make provision for extra discounts which may have been obtained as well as depreciation for slow-selling or slightly soiled stock.

Stocktaking is part of the art of successful bookselling—I could have written retailing—but it is much more an art in bookselling than in most forms of retailing as the number of new books each year is so very high and their individual lives can be short, so whereas depreciation is a factor always to be reckoned with in retailing it is specially important in bookselling.

With every system of stocktaking known to me it is usual to see that all fixtures or shelves, display stands or tables, etc., bear a number. Do not forget the windows! If shelves are numbered this requires an annual check, as numbers may get removed during the course of a year or need alteration owing to structural changes.

As regards bad stock, in the case of the average-size general bookshop it is suggested that the best method is for competent people to go along each shelf in advance of stocktaking and remove every book which is unlikely to sell at the full price within a reasonable time.

The remaining stock on the shelves can then be totalled at selling price and reduced to approximate cost price, as I have explained. If old stock has been removed, this method gives an accurate value, but only in bookshops stocking mainly up-to-date general books.

Books which have been removed from the shelves as being worth less than the cost, or of no value, should be written off or reduced in price. If reduced in value they should be included in the stock figures at the marked-down value. This reduced value should not be more than the price at which it is estimated the books can be sold at a 50 per cent 'mark-up' (that is, half on the revised 'cost'). Particulars of all stock 'written off' or 'written down' should be recorded for audit purposes. A list of titles, published prices, number of copies, totalled at the original cost followed by the reduced cost, may be required but as this stock is usually not worth much there is little point in wasting time on it; you can simply take down the published prices on the roll of an adding machine. Mark the roll 'Books removed from shelves "No Value"' or 'Taken into stock at 25p each' or some other nominal figure.

If stocktaking is done in this way the total figure arrived at is likely to approximate to the real value, but it does not follow that all books reduced at cost must be *sold* at reduced prices. They can be returned to the shelves and given a further chance to sell at the full published prices, provided, that is, that in each book a reduced price in code is noted to prevent its being entered on the stock sheets at full price in the following stocktaking. The common practice is to return to the shelves some books reduced in cost—those which are 'probables'—and to offer the remainder in the National Book Sale at reduced prices. Stocktaking dealt with in this manner need have no terrors; but this simple method cannot be used in many types of business, such as University and other specialized bookshops, as the stock is more complex and vulnerable, so often the more orthodox method of *listing stock* is necessary.

When listing every book in stock there are a few practical ways of simplifying the actual work. First, as already mentioned, check to see that each tier or shelf is properly numbered. Secondly, adopt a method of getting stock together to reduce the number of items which have to be listed. The method depends on the size of the stock and possibly on other considerations. If every book on every shelf is to be detailed on to stock sheets, the number of sheets required can be very large and the entering, checking and totalling will be a big task. So to reduce the volume, first sort into price order all books on every shelf or if you wish in every tier. This speeds up the work at stocktaking, although there is the disadvantage that for a day or two staff engaged in selling may find it difficult to locate particular titles. Let me try to make the system clear by instancing a classification, say fiction; for stock-taking purposes the whole section can first be rearranged on the shelves in price order, starting at the most expensive and going down to the cheapest—instead of the usual author and title arrangement. It will be seen that the number of stock titles can then be reduced simply to so many at say £2.00 and so many at £1.50 and so on.

The alternative of leaving stock in its usual alphabetical position in each section on the shelves and entering it item by item will necessitate many more entries for each shelf, but in very large concerns the above rearrangement of stock suggested is inconvenient or impossible. When the time comes for the final check, hours of work are saved by the method described, but many firms must rely on the orthodox listing of every book in their order on the shelves, using date coding to arrive at a separate total for first year, second year, third year and older stock.

From such consolidated records it is possible to arrive at a total stock figure after writing down the retail value of the stock according to age, and several bookshops consider that a 40 per cent reduction on selling price for the first-year book, 60 per cent for the second-year, 80 per cent for the third-year and a complete write-off for older stock gives a balanced valuation of the stock held. One advantage of this system, particularly in academic bookselling, is the ability to see from year to year whether increasing proportions of second, third and older stocks, are being built up, indicating that unsold stock is not being returned efficiently to publishers for credit, over-buying is occurring and not enough use is being made of the National Book Sale facilities to turn older stock into cash.

A bookseller often knows months or even weeks after purchase that certain books are unlikely to sell, and it is unwise to take these into stock at too high a price. Some stock, even some purchased in the current year, will almost always need deduction or depreciation. Hard and fast rules for stocktaking cannot be laid down as so much depends on an individual business.

Booksellers with a large University or Technical trade, or a Library trade together with a large General trade have special problems to overcome. Obviously it is impossible in such businesses to weed out the old stock prior to stocktaking as I have advocated or to regroup stock in price order to the degree suggested for less complicated and smaller businesses, but one or other of the systems outlined in this chapter can be adapted to meet most needs.

Sheets for stocktaking may be ruled up in a variety of ways according to the system used. A very exact way of recording stock is obtained by having ruled stock sheets as follows:

Shelf number	Number of copies	Title	1st Year Publ. prices	2nd Year Publ. prices	3rd Year Publ. prices	Older than 3 years Publ. prices
			£	£	£	£
		Totals				

To obtain a valuation, the first columns, 'First-year stock' are totalled and reduced to 'cost' by deducting 40 per cent. The figures in the second columns definitely need a larger deduction of about 60 per cent and those in the third columns should be reduced by 80 per cent or to nil.

The books reduced to nil should, it is suggested, have the original cost marks erased or crossed through immediately after stocktaking and the 'nil' sign inserted to avoid the possibility of written-off stock being taken into stock at the original cost or some other price at a subsequent stocktaking. These old books can then be sold at the prices they will fetch, always ensuring, of course, that the requirements of the Net Book Agreement are observed.

Another method is to take stock at cost, but this entails putting the cost price in code in every book and this practice takes time and is costly in labour, so it is disappearing, particularly in large shops with quick turnover, but it is the best system in Second-hand and Antiquarian bookselling.

A simple form as shown below (roneoed or printed) is adequate, particularly for small businesses. Each sheet is brought to a total. After stock is checked and sheets totalled, a recapitulation sheet (one giving totals taken from all sheets and added to give a grand total) can be made out and an extra 10 per cent, 15 per cent or more deducted for depreciation according to the year of purchase.

Shelf number	Number of copies	Title	*Cost price	Year of purchase	£	
						Total

* This method is possible only if a code mark representing the date of purchase is made in all books on arrival before they go to the shelves. Otherwise stock must be listed at published prices.

Immediately before stocktaking all 'On Sale' books should, as far as possible, be returned in time for credits to arrive to clear the books. Then the invoice and credit can go through the accounts at the same time.

Finally I stress that the system mentioned earlier in this chapter, of totalling the selling prices by using adding machines, is, in my view, the best for many general booksellers. It is simple and speedy but is not suitable for all. Indeed, if applied in a large business where the stock includes large sections of Technical and Scientific Books, Educational Books and Academic Books, the stock figure would tend to be ridiculously high as such books can all too quickly become out-of-date and of little value irrespective of published price and cost.

The usual time for stocktaking is that time of the year when the stock is likely to be at its lowest. This varies, but in most cases will be 31 January or 31 March.

Remember that over-valuation is unwise, the result being a higher profit on the balance sheet (on which tax will have to be paid), and a day of reckoning will inevitably come.

13

Tools of the Trade

Adequate knowledge and profound interest in what are frequently described as the 'tools of the trade', i.e. Reference Books, are of fundamental importance to success in bookselling. The instruction of beginners in the use of the main reference books is the early responsibility of bookseller-managers and senior assistants. Every assistant must clearly understand the contents of the important reference books and the way to use the book lists which appear in the trade press. In this chapter I give details of the most important reference books and of periodicals used by booksellers.

British Books in Print: no bookshop should be without these two volumes published annually by J. Whitaker & Sons Ltd. This reference catalogue of current literature lists for easy reference all British Books in print, and other books in English if stocked in England. It details author, title, editor, translator, reviser, year of publication or year of latest edition. Number of edition, ISBN, number of pages, illustrations, series, binding where not cloth, price, whether net or non-net, and publisher's name. It is in two volumes, Vol. 1, A–J; Vol. 2, K–Z. It also contains a list of Publishers and their addresses, Publishers Overseas, Agents and Representative.

The Bookseller has long been the unrivalled source of information about the British Book Trade. It is published weekly. Each issue contains a *Complete List of the Week's Publications* and the reprints published; these appear in an alphabetical arrangement under both author and title. These weekly lists are for easy reference put together each month in the publication, *Whitaker's Books of the Month and Books to Come*. This is a valuable time-saver as it provides, at the end of each month, in one inclusive list, not only the cumulated record of the month's books but a record of forthcoming books during the next two months, constantly up-dated month by month.

The Bookseller goes still further and gathers together all the items in the weekly lists in alphabetical order and issues them quarterly. These quarterly references are called *Whitaker's Cumulative Book Lists*. These are invaluable for quick references in every bookshop. *Whitaker's Cumulative Book Lists* record in two separate lists, the first classified under subjects, the second, alphabetical under author, title and subject, all the books in the three months January to March (three months' books), January to June (six months' books), January to September (nine months' books) and then annually *Whitaker's Cumulative Book List* volume for the year, which is a complete record of British Book Production. We in Britain are not only blessed with these fine reference books but to make things even easier we have in addition periodically cumulated volumes of *Whitaker's Cumulative Book List*: five-year Cumulative Book List 1939–1943 (facsimile reprint); four-year Cumulative Book List 1944–1947 (facsimile reprint); five-year Cumulative Book List 1963–1967, and now annually *British Books in Print* (Formerly the *Reference Catalogue of Current Literature*), as detailed above.

Special mention must also be made of the tremendously useful and important Export Numbers of *The Bookseller* (Spring and Autumn), which give very full particulars not only of books published but of *forthcoming* titles during these periods. As the books advertised by the publishers are indexed under title as well as author the Export Numbers present a quick reference.

Paperbacks in Print. This is issued at six to nine months' intervals. It is arranged in two sections. In the first, entries are arranged alphabetically by authors under subject and in the second, in alphabetical sequence of authors and titles.

Technical and Scientific Books in Print, published annually, details more than 25,000 titles in the pure and applied sciences.

Books are listed by author, by title and also under 45 headings and 300 sub-classifications. Bibliographical details are also given. Addresses are given of publishers whose books are included.

Children's Books in Print, issued annually, is arranged in two sections, alphabetically by authors under subject and secondly in alphabetical sequence of authors and titles.

My desk companion over many years which saves hours and costs only a moderate sum is a cloth-bound booklet, *Publishers in the United Kingdom and Their Addresses*, which is extracted from *British Books in Print*. It, too, is issued annually and includes telephone numbers and other useful information. *The Bookseller* and all the publications to which I have referred are issued by J. Whitaker & Son Ltd, 13 Bedford Square, London WC1B 3JE.

Smith's Trade News is published weekly by W. H. Smith & Son Ltd, Strand House, Portugal Street, London WC2A 2HS. This contains notes and news of books. Their special children's book number, issued in August annually, is particularly useful. Smith's Trade News is exceptionally valuable to booksellers who are also stationers and newsagents.

The British National Bibliography is a central cataloguing and bibliographical service, edited at the British Museum and published by the Council of the British National Bibliography Ltd, 7 Rathbone Street, London W1P 2AL. *The British National Bibliography* is the most complete record of British publishing. It is also the most informative. Based on the books received at the British Museum, where all copies of new British publications are deposited, it contains much elusive material recorded for the first time. The entries are prepared by qualified bibliographers from actual copies of the books. All statements are carefully checked with original sources in the library of the British Museum. Helpful bibliographical details as to size, number of pages, illustrations and previous editions, as well as the publisher and price, are given, and a detailed analysis of the subject-matter of each book is systematically presented. The full service offered by *The British National Bibliography* provides a weekly list of current publications arranged by both subject and author, with a cumulated author, title and subject index every month; quarterly cumulations cover the periods January to March, January to June, January to September, so that each cumulation supersedes the others; and a cloth-bound annual volume. In addition a cumulated author, title and subject index to the first five annual volumes and a cumulated subject catalogue of the years 1951–1954 are available. For the bookseller the complete and authoritative weekly issues, with their subject arrangement and full bibliographical details of each item, make the compilation of subject lists an easy matter. With very little trouble up-to-date information can be issued regularly to specialist customers, bringing valuable business. Customers' own inquiries can be just as easily satisfied. Books written on any subject or by any writer can be traced in a matter of seconds. From the slimmest monograph to the many-volume encyclopaedia, both trade and non-trade publications, everything is recorded in *The British National Bibliography*.

Everyone working in a bookshop should have at least a thorough working knowledge of the reference books mentioned, and of course the trade press, which includes *Bookselling News* issued free to members of the Booksellers Association, is also full of interesting articles, items of news, announcements and advertisements. These reference books and periodicals are of primary importance, but booksellers use an enormous range of reference books many of which will almost certainly form part of the stock for sale on the shelves. So a bookseller's reference book can be divided into three main categories:

(a) Those he has to purchase, which are produced for the trade.
(b) Publishers' lists and catalogues, which are available gratis.
(c) Books which are part of the bookseller's stocks and are published for general sale, such as *Who's Who* and *Whitaker's Almanack*, Encyclopaedias, etc.

Almost every book is to some extent a reference book, because information about a publisher's books frequently appear on the jacket, and other titles by the author are commonly detailed on the fly-leaf or on the jacket. Many books contain important bibliographies and some of them are mentioned below.

The first in importance for booksellers is, perhaps *Who's Who*, which gives under the names of important living authors particulars of their published works in chronological order, with the dates of the first issue. *Who Was Who* and *The Concise Dictionary of National Biography* contain brief biographies and details of the writings of famous authors. A point which needs emphasis is that *Who's Who* deals with living authors and, of course, other prominent people, but *The Concise Dictionary of National Biography* includes also those no longer living. To these two important reference books must be added *Chambers's Biographical Dictionary*, which contains details of the lives and works of writers of all nations, whereas the two former references cover only the British Isles.

Other reference books which may be in the bookseller's stock and which contain bibliographies or other useful information include the following:

Cambridge History of Literature.
Chambers's Encyclopaedia.
Encyclopaedia Britannica.
Oxford Companion to English Literature.
Oxford Dictionary of Quotations.
Everyman's Encyclopaedia.
Readers' Guide to the World's Greatest Books—this gives in one alphabetical sequence names of all authors and titles in the Everyman's Library and provides bibliographical details. It is published by J. M. Dent Ltd, 26 Albemarle Street, London W1.
The Statesman's Year Book.
Whitaker's Almanack includes, among a wealth of useful material, a list of societies and institutions, which is invaluable when applying for lists of members to whom it is proposed to send specialized catalogues or prospectuses.

Valuable books of reference for booksellers dealing in Children's Books include:

Intent upon Reading, Margery Fisher's critical appraisal of modern fiction for children and the companion volume *Matters of Fact,* both published by the Brockhampton Press.

The Who's Who of Children's Literature, compiled and edited by Brian Doyle, gives authors and illustrators of their books, arranged alphabetically, 400 names with biographical, bibliographical and background details covering a comprehensive list of British, American and European contributors, from 1800 to the present day, published by Hugh Evelyn & Sons Ltd.

British Children's Books in the 20th Century, by Frank Eyre, a standard study of modern children's books published in Longman's Young Books.

Booksellers should also know of the existence of the following important reference books which are used by large businesses or specialist bookshops.

Wilson's Cumulative Book Index is one of the most important references published. It is an author–title–subject index to books recently published in the English language anywhere in the world. Government publications, music, pamphlets and miniature editions are excluded, as are works which are wholly in a foreign language; dictionaries, grammars, phrase-books, readers, editions of foreign classics, and other aids to language learning are included if they contain some English. An accurate and comprehensive list, it is particularly useful for location of books when only a part of the bibliographic information is available.

Each book listed in *Cumulative Book Index* is always classified under as many subject headings as its contents require. Subject entries include author's or editor's name, full title of the book, publisher, publication date and price. Each issue also contains a directory of publishers and distributors.

Cumulative Book Index is published monthly, except August, with quarterly cumulations and a permanent annual volume. Full particulars can be obtained from the agents in Britain, W. & R. Holmes (Books), 98–100 Holm Street, Glasgow G26 SN.

Permanent Volumes in Print:
 Five-year volume: 1928–1932
 Five-year volume: 1933–1937
 Five-year volume: 1938–1942

Six-year volume: 1943–1948
Four-year volume: 1949–1952
Four-year volume: 1953–1956
Two-year volume: 1957–1958
Two-year volume: 1959–1960
Two-year volume: 1961–1962
Two-year volume: 1963–1964
Two-year volume: 1965–1966
Two-year volume: 1967–1968
One-year volume: 1969
One-year volume: 1970
One-year volume: 1971

Books in Print USA lists all current available USA titles and is published annually by R. F. Bowker Co, New York (London office: Bowker Publishing Co Ltd, 18 Bedford Row, London WC1R 4EJ). It records American books in print up to the previous July and is arranged in two volumes. The first lists titles alphabetically by author and the second lists titles in alphabetical order. A third volume, *Subject Guide to Books in Print*, lists all the titles under subject headings.

The American Book Publishing Record, Annual Cumulatives. Published annually by Bowker and cumulates all the books listed in the previous twelve monthly issues of the *American Book Publishing Record.* Every five years these are cumulated into a multi-volume five-year cumulative.

Compiled and edited by Robin Myers in association with the National Book League, *A Dictionary of Literature in the English Language from Chaucer to 1940*, is in two volumes. Volume 1 is an alphabetical arrangement under authors, giving a brief bibliographical note, an indication of bibliographic sources used or recommended, followed by a list of first editions in chronological order. Volume 2 is a complete title–author index of the 60,000 works to facilitate further easy access to the information in the main volume.

A Guide to the Best Fiction, English and American, including translations from foreign languages, by Ernest A. Baker and James Packman.

An English Library is an annotated list of classics and standard books by F. Seymour Smith, FLA (published by André Deutsch in association with the National Book League). Also by the same author, *Bibliography in the Bookshop.*

The Author's and Writer's Who's Who (Burke's Peerage Ltd) gives over 10,000 biographies of living writers—British, Commonwealth, American and foreign writers whose works have been translated into English. Full bibliographical information is given, including titles of books and their publishers, so that author, book title and publisher are linked together in one entry. Biographies appear also of journalists, editors and critics, with their staff appointments.

Book Auction Records are used mainly by the antiquarian book trade. They give prices obtained and full particulars of books sold at auction. Published annually by Dawsons of Pall Mall (see page 126) and cumulated every five years.

BPRA Handbook, issued by the Book Publishers' Representatives Association, is a list of members with their addresses and the firms they represent.

British Initials and Abbreviations, published by Leonard Hill (Books), Intertext House, 24 Market Square, Aylesbury, Bucks. A list of all organizations in Great Britain and Ireland with international organizations connected with Britain on a governmental, institutional or individual level. This list is arranged alphabetically according to the organizations' initials.

Cumulated Fiction Index by G. B. Cotton and Alan Glencross. This publication is better known to librarians than to booksellers, but it is one of the best reference books imaginable. It is the only contemporary British work of its kind and enables one to trace novels in any subject or in any location or period of history. (Obtainable from the Association of Assistant Librarians, Public Library, Falkirk, Stirling.)

Lewis's Library Catalogues contain details of scientific, technical and medical books, with a subject index.

National Book League Catalogue of the Library is a catalogue of books about books.

National Book League Lists and other publications are useful for their bibliographies, etc.

Sharp's Dictionary of English Authors is an old reference book. It is particularly useful for the dates of first editions.

Sonnenschein Best Books, in six volumes, is an old reference book, but it is an invaluable guide for classification.

Willing's Press Guide, issued annually, is a comprehensive Index and Handbook of the Press of the United Kingdom of Great Britain, Northern Ireland and the Irish Republic together with the principal Commonwealth publications. It is published by Thomas Skinner Directories, RAC House, Lansdowne Road, Croydon CR9 2HE.

Writers' and Artists' Year Book (A. & C. Black Ltd) is a directory for writers, artists, playwrights, film writers, photographers and composers. It is a valuable reference book for booksellers, containing a reference section giving details of copyright and an outline of the law of libel, publishers' agreements, the writer and income-tax liability, indexes, etc. It also gives a list of pseudonyms, a classified index of journals and magazines, sizes of books, type faces, signs used in correcting proofs, etc. It is revised annually.

To these must be added books which deal more specifically with the trade itself, including:

Cassell's Directory of Publishing in Great Britain, the Commonwealth, Ireland and South Africa, contains much useful information including publishing and allied trades associations and agencies, book societies and book clubs, literary foundations as well as authors' agents, commercial artists, lecture agents, photo agencies, etc.

Clegg's International Directory of the World's Book Trade, an irregular publication issued by James Clarke & Co Ltd, 7 All Saints Passage, Cambridge CB2 3LS.

Directory of Dealers in Secondhand and Antiquarian Books in the British Isles, issued annually (Sheppard Press Ltd, PO Box 42, 15 James's Street, London WC2E 8BX). This is an extremely useful, up-to-date guide containing detailed information about over 800 dealers, as well as other information.

Trade Associations and Professional Bodies of the United Kingdom,

published by the Pergamon Press, Headington Hill Hall, Oxford
(orders to Book Centre Ltd, Rufford Road, Southport, Lancs),
is divided into four parts:

(i) An alphabetical list of Trade Associations and Professional
Bodies.
(ii) A geographical index to Associations listed in Part I which
are outside the Greater London Area.
(iii) A list of Chambers of Trade, Commerce and Shipping
together with the UK offices of Chambers of Commerce.
(iv) An alphabetical list of the UK offices of International Bodies.

Finally there are the trade and literary papers, which include
The Bookseller and *Smith's Trade News*, already mentioned and
other important newspapers and periodicals including:

Book Addict, issued monthly from Wesley–Dunne Publications
Ltd, 58B London Road, Kingston upon Thames, Surrey.
Books and Bookmen, a monthly publication published by
Hansom Books Ltd.
British Book News, published by the British Council.
The Clique, issued weekly for second-hand antiquarian book-
sellers. It consists mainly of columns of 'Books Wanted' by the
trade and is published by Clique Ltd, 109 Wembley Park Drive,
Middlesex HA9 8HG.

The Listener.
The New Statesman.
The Observer.
The Spectator.
The Sunday Telegraph.
The Sunday Times.
Time and Tide.
The Times Literary Supplement.

Other than the trade papers and English catalogues referred to
at the beginning, however, the most important aids for the bookseller are the publishers' catalogues and announcement lists.
It is not necessary nor possible to include a complete list of

books which serve as references in a bookshop, but those mentioned will cover the requirements of most booksellers.

Not only is knowledge of the contents of reference books of paramount importance for good bookselling, but equally important are easy accessibility of reference books and their careful replacement after use. Care in handling them is stressed, as many are expensive and rather heavy for the covers; if handled carelessly they will soon disintegrate. When pages of a valuable reference book become loose, or the whole book is loose in the covers, send it to the binder for immediate repair. He will usually oblige and make it a 'rush job' as he understands that such books are in constant use. Even the inexpensive reference books, or those which cost nothing, should be replaced and treated with care. Publishers' catalogues, for instance, should not have pieces cut out of them to provide customers with details, unless another copy is immediately available to replace the incomplete one.

14

Second-hand Bookselling

Bookshops can be roughly classified as follows. Those offering new books only, paperbacks and hardbacks; second-hand books only; new and second-hand books; new books with periodicals and stationery; and there are combinations of all these, some with side-lines including newsagencies, post offices, fancy goods, etc. The selling of second-hand books is commonly linked with the selling of new books, but some classification of second-hand books is needed to avoid confusion.

Second-hand books include:

Antiquarian. That is, rare and valuable early printed books, rare editions, first editions, etc.

Specialist Books. Sellers of second-hand books specialize more than sellers of new books. There are specialists in most subjects, natural history, anthropology, travel, history, art, theology, limited and first editions, to mention a few.

General Books. The largest group. Many sellers of second-hand books have a general stock but specialize to some extent in certain subjects.

The selling of second-hand books is not only an important branch of bookselling; it is also often considered to be the most remunerative. Why then do not more booksellers add this side to their businesses? One reason doubtless is that few understand the trade. Many booksellers know little about the buying and selling of second-hand books—they know enough of the book trade generally to realize that there must be a good deal of specialized knowledge required, and not possessing it hesitate to launch out.

It is true that a knowledge of second-hand bookselling can be acquired only the hard way—by experience. It is a more specialized business than selling new books, and although *both* are lifetime studies, a sufficient working knowledge of the *new* book trade can be acquired in a reasonable time. A truly sound knowledge of the antiquarian book business can be obtained only by many years' actual experience in bookshops dealing in rare books, by study and by contacts with those who know the trade.

Some guidance for beginners, particularly in the more general side of selling second-hand books, can, however, be given in a book of this nature. It is, in fact, from small beginnings—the buying and selling of a few lots of second-hand books—that many booksellers have gradually acquired knowledge of book values and the business methods which particularly apply to second-hand bookselling. In course of time they have widened the scope of their businesses and flourished.

For beginners the common-sense methods must be adhered to for steady progress. Any bookseller can, by putting a notice in his shop window, or by advertisement, make it known that he is open to buy second-hand books, and books will very soon be offered to him, from single copies to complete libraries, but he must be on his guard not to buy stolen books as he may be in trouble as a 'receiver'.

It must be the immediate aim of anyone wishing to build up a connection with the book-buying public and the second-hand book trade to endeavour to satisfy customers' requirements. It is not sufficient to be self-complacent about the items in stock and expect to prosper from customers buying merely from the window or from the shelves. A lot of business is done by reporting items to those likely to be interested in buying them. The various reading and collecting tastes of individuals are quickly assessed in second-hand bookselling, and an attempt to meet these requirements must be made at the outset. Not only are certain subjects and particular titles in those classifications asked for, but somewhat vague inquiries are received. Some customers might ask for a book giving habits of dogs, fishes or Buddhist monks;

others might want a large-type Bible or a pocket edition of Kipling. Your knowledge of books and your service will be tested every hour of the day by customers endeavouring to obtain books on subjects in which they are particularly interested.

It is important that the customer should not simply be told, 'I am very sorry, I have not a copy', when a book is not in stock. It should be realized that he *wants* the book, so it is better to offer to try to find a copy for him. This shows the bookseller's keenness and interest, and when his offer to try to obtain the book is accepted he will get the name and address of the customer for future reference.

Booksellers usually advertise their customers' 'wants' in a trade paper that is available weekly to booksellers dealing in second-hand books. They customarily include in their 'wants' list books they will buy for stock.

A book advertised for a customer will not usually result in a good profit, as expenses are heavy. It will cost quite a few pence for advertising each title and extra costs include postage on a card ordering the book, postage to advise the customer, poundage on the postal order to pay for the book, and postage to settle the invoice, plus the cost of stationery. At least some of his overhead costs must be added to the price asked of the customer for the book to make a fair profit as well as the profit margin of at least half on cost.

This over-simplification of a small transaction is given to show the cost of pleasing a customer and building up goodwill. In practice costs can be much heavier than those given above, for instance, it may be necessary to advertise several times before a copy of the required book is offered. Then, when the person who asked for the book is notified, he may reply that he no longer required it, as he has already found one, or the copy is too expensive. Although all this must be taken into consideration it is unwise to over-price books as customers will not return if your competitors sell more cheaply. Always have a few bargains on your shelves to encourage people to call in and browse. It should be realized at the outset that it is not enough for anyone to obtain a stock of second-hand books, put them on the shelves of a shop, and start up in business, in the hope that he will succeed as a second-hand book dealer; this searching for books for customers is an integral part of the business.

Although it is strongly recommended that beginners should first get experience with some good firm, or alternatively employ an experienced person, many successful booksellers have started from scratch. Common sense goes a long way.

An essential element in the life of a dealer in second-hand books is to call in and browse around other bookshops, not only to pick up bargains but to chat and exchange information with competitors. A great deal can be 'picked up' in these friendly chats about prices and demand.

The trade in second-hand books differs from that in new books mainly in that it covers books published during five or more centuries. It is evident that not only does it give wide scope, but it also requires an encyclopaedic knowledge, which is gained by handling books on all subjects, buying and selling them, and by a continuous concentration and delving into bibliographical works, booksellers' catalogues, sale catalogues and records of books and prices of all kinds.

An important feature of the second-hand business is the buying and selling of books between members of the trade. Some booksellers do a large part of their business by reporting items from their stock to the booksellers advertising in the 'Books Wanted' columns of *The Clique* and other trade journals. Always welcome fellow booksellers who call on you—it pays!

Valuing and pricing

If a newcomer to the trade cannot value the books offered because he has insufficient knowledge, what is the best procedure? First, he should not take large risks. If there is any doubt as to the value of books offered, it is wise not to make a firm offer. If a collection or library is offered and the bookseller feels certain it is good, but cannot value it, a wise course would be to call in a fellow bookseller who is competent to judge. For a commission, or some other arrangement to mutual advantage, he may be willing to assist and so be instrumental in making a purchase which eventually results in a profitable transaction.

The beginner should always be on the alert to learn as quickly as possible which books are likely to appeal to the specialist booksellers. By selling quickly to the trade a profitable business can be built up and a bookseller can at the same time develop sections in his own shop, particularly those he knows something about. In the case of a shop previously selling new books only, the knowledge obtained in that trade would obviously be useful to some extent in developing the second-hand side to the business, but the beginner is urged to 'tread warily'. For instance, if he has a business dealing in new fiction and popular non-fiction, he may decide that it is possible to sell similar books second-hand, and no doubt he could do so, but it is unlikely that he will be able to sell such books at other than low prices, so he cannot pay much when buying for stock. At first it is perhaps advisable to proceed on the assumption that it is possible to pay half the price that is expected to be obtained. That will cover an allowance for the books which do not sell.

This is not to say that all second-hand book dealers pay only half the ultimate selling price of the books. Many specialist booksellers have such regular trade that they can pay excellent prices for their type of book and may work roughly at the same margin as dealers in new books, that is, half added on to cost or a little more.

Other factors—the original selling prices, condition, etc.—are also important to the fixing of a selling price. A point to be stressed is that the higher the value of a book, the higher may be the proportionate purchasing price. For example, where a firm might buy at roughly 'half selling price' for general stock, they could pay more for a book of value for which there is a quick sale; for instance, if a book sells readily at £20 it would not be advisable to offer only £10 for it. At £15 it may still be a worthwhile transaction. Buying at £80 a *quick-selling book* selling for £100 is better business than making an offer of £50 which is not accepted, but if it is a book which may possibly be on the shelves a long time and will need cataloguing it is necessary to make 40 or 50 per cent or more on the cost price.

A good buying reputation should be aimed at, and a help towards this is to pay fair prices.

Sound business method is all-important in the building up of a second-hand book business. Slipshod methods are likely to prove disastrous. When making an offer for books, the bookseller should first place a value on each one he thinks he can sell, and either refuse any others offered, or quote a very small figure for them. It is, of course, not necessary to let the person from whom books are being bought know how much will be allowed on each one, but it is important that, when the transaction is completed, the actual cost price should be marked in code in each book. A bookseller who gives a rather hasty glance at a collection offered to him, and then makes an offer which he thinks the customer will accept, and having purchased the books merely marks selling prices in them, is obviously not doing his job properly and will not be able to ascertain the true position at stocktaking. On the other hand, a bookseller who puts the actual cost price in code in each book and sees that every volume for which nothing was actually paid also carries a code mark to indicate nil, will be able to see how far his valuations have proved correct, and to ascertain the profit or loss figure.

If you watch a skilled book-valuer at work you will see that in the case of a library he values every book, possibly making a a list as he goes along of the titles and the amount he is prepared to pay for them. He usually works in code when pricing, and with practice he is able to use code letters instead of figures and arrive at a total without difficulty. In the case of a library where there are not many important items, he may appear to place a value on each shelf of books, but in actual fact he will also have carefully examined every book on the shelf, so there is no guess-work about it.

From time to time a valuer may take a book from the shelves because he is not absolutely certain of its value, and after having valued all the books with which he is familiar, he will then sit down with his catalogues to ascertain the values of unfamiliar books. However large or small a library or collection of books, the method is in essence always the same. Every book is valued individually, and after purchase the cost prices are written in each volume in code, and any books which are obtained for nothing are marked with the code indicating nil. This latter is important, as in the purchase of collections and libraries invariably there are a number of books which may possibly be sold at small prices, but on which nothing has been allowed, as they are not regarded as being good items for stock. Some of these items are possibly placed in a case or box outside the shop. High-class booksellers not wishing to include such books as part of their stock may sell them to other booksellers who can dispose of them.

Costing and Pricing

To give a clearer picture of the method of costing books accurately let us assume a bookseller has been called to see a collection of books at the house of one of his customers and after careful examination he has worked out that he can afford to pay the sum of £25 for them. He makes this offer and it is accepted. It is then his business to arrange for the collection of the books and, to be on the safe side, he will doubtless have made notes regarding those on which he has placed a value, and possibly counted the total number of volumes. When the stock is received, the number of volumes is checked and the titles of the important ones checked against the notes made. The sum of £25 has now to be allocated. It frequently happens that the bookseller, on further examination, wishes to adjust the original costings, but whatever adjustments are made the total cost prices put in the books must be the amount paid for the collection. There are many methods of arranging the books before costing, and a familiar one is to place in piles books which are to be costed at certain prices, e.g. one pile of books to be costed at £1 per volume, another at 75p, another at 50p, and so on. Alternatively, and particularly in the case of rare and more valuable books, the notes and values made at the time of valuation can be used as an invoice. As each book is found it is priced and a line run through the item on the notes.

For further identification of items it is a common practice to include code marks which give not only the cost price but also the year of purchase and a means of knowing from whom the book was actually purchased. This may at first sound complicated, but it is in fact a very simple process. A special record book is kept in which are entered the vendor's name, address and the total amount paid for each purchase. The first collection bought in the year is number 1, the second number 2, and so on throughout the year. If we assume that the purchase to which we have referred above was the thirty-fifth of the year, a coded price might appear as follows:

$$\frac{C/-/-}{35/73} \text{ or } \frac{C/X/X}{35/73}$$

Here we are using the word CUMBERLAND as a code, details of which are given on page 50, and the letter X to indicate nil. If the coded prices are placed in all the books purchased, it is obvious that on taking a book from the shelf one knows at a glance that, for example, it cost £1 and was bought in the year 1973. Reference to the record makes it possible to ascertain the name and address of the customer from whom it was purchased.

These references are invaluable in a variety of ways, particularly if the books are stolen from the shop, or if the purchases included some that have been stolen elsewhere. In the ordinary course of business, however, this coding is a necessary safeguard. If the bookseller employs a buyer, he can obviously, from time to time, check the prices he is paying by simply picking up books at random and seeing if the costs are sound.

When books have been marked with the cost price they will also have to be marked with the selling price. This may sometimes be done at the same time, but more frequently the costing is one process and the marking of the selling price another. Where a good system operates, it is even possible to allow a junior to mark the actual cost prices in code in the books, working from lists supplied by the valuer, but an experienced bookseller will naturally have to mark the selling prices. The selling price of a popular book still in print would, of course, be dependent on the published price of the book, the condition, the demand and the supply. For a book published at 75p it may be possible to ask 50p for a fine second-hand copy, but if there is little demand for it, it may have to be priced as low as 25p or even lower. The correct pricing of second-hand books comes with experience, but the bookseller cannot go far wrong if he sells the majority of the second-hand books purchased at double the cost price or at least half added on to cost or more; that is to say, a book for which he has paid 25p may be marked 50p or at least 45p. Slow-selling titles frequently carry a much larger mark-up. The bookseller may have paid only 10p for a book but he may price it at 50p because he knows it will be worth that to a buyer, if he can find one. As there is small demand for the title, however, he may have to keep it for some considerable time before a buyer is found—in fact, much of this type of stock is never sold at all.

One can give only rough hints on valuation and pricing of books. All booksellers study the catalogues and prices in other booksellers' lists as a guide to values. Many factors affect prices— condition, edition, whether the book is still in print, and always the two most important factors, supply and demand. Books out of print may be priced as high as the original published price, and sometimes very much more, depending upon their scarcity and the demand for them. Books are published which help with the identification of first editions and scarce books. There are, for instance, the *Book Auction Records*, the bibliographies of famous authors, and the catalogues of the great libraries, but undoubtedly the most valuable guides are the *Book Auction Records* and the catalogues of reliable booksellers. Items of particular interest to the trade include first and limited editions, books which bear inscriptions and signatures of authors, rare books on a variety of subjects, topography, travel, oriental, history, early printed books, particularly *Incunabula*[1] and so on. If there is a book that is thought to be valuable, it can always be offered to a reliable bookseller who specializes and who will make a fair offer for it; or it may, of course, be placed in one of the book auctions.

[1] Incunabula: books printed before AD 1501.

Catalogues

The issuing of catalogues of second-hand books and the building up of mailing lists are also an integral part of the second-hand book business. Libraries of all kinds, as well as private collectors and, of course, booksellers themselves, are all buyers of worthwhile books.

Before he begins to compile a catalogue the bookseller is advised to study the catalogues of competitors. They tend to follow a pattern, but cataloguing is an art and booksellers aim to provide more than just a list of authors, titles and prices. The reading of a catalogue should give pleasure as well as information and an occasional illustration, although costly, adds charm and usually pays off. The usual method of arrangement is: number of item, name of author, initials, title, size, binding, publication date, price and the *condition* of each item. Items may be sorted into various classifications. One thing to bear in mind in preparing a catalogue of second-hand books is the fact that there is in all probability only one copy of each title for sale, and the amount of space which can be devoted to inexpensive items must necessarily be small, as printing is costly.

Catalogues of books on specialized subjects, addressed discriminately, will almost certainly be found to be more profitable than catalogues of miscellaneous books. In the former case of specialized books it is likely that some particular organization or society will provide a list of members to whom catalogues can be addressed.

There is much to be said for specialization. Once a bookseller is known to specialize in certain subjects he will receive not only requests from customers interested in those subjects but will in all probability be offered libraries and collections of books by specialist collectors. Trade buyers interested in similar classes of books will also contact him from time to time.

Classification

Second-hand books are, in the main, arranged on the shelves in the same way as new books; they are placed in various classifications under the names of the authors. Everyone familiar with bookshops dealing with second-hand books will have observed that many of them are very untidy and overcrowded. The reason for this is the tendency to accumulate large stocks for which there is slow demand. Much of the stock will in all probability sell ultimately, but as the demand is small little will no doubt have been paid for the stock so that the bookseller can afford to wait for buyers to come along. It is obviously not possible to pay a high price for books which must wait on the shelves perhaps for years before they can be sold. To some extent this is not appreciated by customers who can be disappointed when selling books which they bought new at the total published price of, say, £30 and are offered perhaps £5 for the lot. The offer is quite likely to be a very fair one, or indeed generous, as the books may have been published a long time ago, and the demand for them may be no longer keen.

In buying books of a specialist nature, such as law, technical and medical books, special care must be exercised, as they tend to be quickly superseded by new and revised editions. In such cases the old editions are frequently valueless.

Libraries of famous people, particularly in learned spheres, are much sought after and a good second-hand book dealer is always in the market for them for several reasons. First, there is the prestige of being able to offer for sale the library of a person of world renown. Secondly, if he is a specialist the whole collection will almost certainly be of particular interest to other specialists in the same field. One frequently finds that the insignificant items in a collection of this nature, for which little cost has been allowed, are quickly snapped up, and the purchase of one such collection very frequently leads to others and perhaps to the beginning of a specialist trade.

Members of the trade should be made welcome and invited to buy from the stock. If a bookseller is making a fair margin of profit, there is no reason why he should not sell to the trade, and there are the advantages that trade buyers will often buy in bulk and will not keep him waiting for the money. Trade buyers and certain libraries usually expect a discount of about 10 per cent off the prices marked in the books, and if their requests as to prices and discounts are reasonable, it will pay to meet them. A smaller profit and quick return will enable more books to be purchased; and very much valuable experience is to be gained in the buying and selling of as many books as possible. From time to time it will doubtless be found necessary for a bookseller to refuse to buy, either because he is overstocked or overspent, or more frequently because so many of the books offered will be those for which there is no great demand. As stocks increase, a buyer must be more selective. On seeing a library or collection he must pick out the volumes he particularly wants and make an offer for them. If the customer is willing only to sell the collection as a whole, it may be better for a bookseller not to purchase.

At stocktaking, the total cost of the volumes remaining on the shelves must be ascertained by totalling the prices in code in each book, and allowing a reasonable amount for depreciation. Publishers' remainders are often included with second-hand books in stock and in catalogues.

If eligible, a bookseller is advised to obtain membership of the Antiquarian Booksellers Association; also membership of The Clique. A proposer and seconder from the trade are necessary requirements in each instance.

Some Overheads

The overheads in second-hand bookselling can be very high and must be watched. A large amount of shelving space is required for a general business, and the amount of detail work entailed requires far more staff than might be supposed. The necessary staff is likely to be costly, not only because of the number required, but because wages paid to experienced assistants with sound training and thorough knowledge of the second-hand book trade are frequently higher than those paid in the new book trade. This is not surprising, when one considers the years the assistants have spent learning the trade and the shortage of experienced people.

The printing of catalogues and cost of postage are heavy items. The cost of printing and paper has gone up considerably in recent years, so the production of a page of a catalogue may work out at several pounds. It will be seen that a small catalogue of 32 pages means a considerable outlay; and the postage on catalogues is costly. Catalogues returned undelivered through the post because of customers having moved and left no forwarding address, etc., mean extra expense for postage, but it enables the mailing list to be kept up to date if they are accepted from the postman, and payment of the surcharge is not a waste of money.

The return of cash in the form of postal orders or cheques when customers have enclosed money with their orders for books that have already been sold, is another expense which mounts up. Correspondence regarding books sold and answers to postal inquiries also entail additional expense.

Many booksellers offer books post free to customers in the British Isles on orders from the catalogue of £5 or more in value. Order forms included in the catalogues, and envelopes to send them out, as well as the cost of labour to address them, are costs which have to be met. The seller of second-hand books has, however, the great advantage of fixing his own selling and cost price subject, of course, to the natural laws of competition. The selling of second-hand books is not easy but it has a fascination of its own.

Chapter 13, 'Tools of the Trade', is primarily devoted to the reference books used by booksellers dealing in new books, although several are equally useful to dealers in second-hand books.

In addition to the books described in Chapter 13 there are a number of reference books particularly important to dealers in second-hand books. The range is a very large one because special bibliographies exist on many authors and numerous subjects.

Generally, however, perhaps the most important reference books are: *The Shorter Dictionary of National Biography*, *The Cambridge Bibliography of English Literature* (Myers), and *A Dictionary of Literature in the English Language*. The latter lists most books of literary merit written in English, arranged alphabetically under the authors with chronological dates of publication of their works, throughout the world. The *Encyclopaedia Britannica* and most other good encyclopaedias are a great help as at the end of each article there is usually a bibliography on the subject.

15

The Booksellers Association of Great Britain and Ireland

The Booksellers Association can be of service to all those who rely in any way on the sale of new books for a living, whether the business is large or small. Throughout its existence the Association has consistently and successfully worked for the improvement of terms and conditions of supply to booksellers, and if ever a trade association justified its existence the Booksellers Association did when, on 30 October 1962—a memorable date—in the Restrictive Practices Court, judgement was delivered on the Net Book Agreement that it was 'not contrary to the public interest'.

This great victory was the direct result of the work of the Booksellers Association together with the Publishers Association, and vindicated their faith and that of the trade in the Net Book Agreement.

The Booksellers Association keeps publishers fully informed of the bookselling point of view, and takes up any matters involving questions of trade practice and principle. It also provides members with various services, which are detailed below.

Objects

The objects for which the Association is established are as follows:
(a) To do anything which the Council may think necessary or desirable for promoting the sale of books, and the promotion and protection of the interests of booksellers, or of members of the Association in relation to their business of dealing in

books (but not including the giving of financial assistance to any member), and particularly, but without limiting the generality of the foregoing.

(b) To improve and maintain the status of the book trade and its relation with other trades and the public, and to improve, or encourage the improvement of, the education and technical qualifications of members and their employees with the object of rendering good service to the community.

(c) To co-operate for mutual benefit with other organizations concerned with the creation, production and distribution of books.

How it is Run

The Booksellers Association has a president (elected annually but who usually serves two terms in office), a vice-president nominated by the Council or the branches, an honorary treasurer, a director and a Council.

Six members of the Council are elected annually by the members at the Annual Conference. There are also fifteen local branches throughout Great Britain and Ireland, each of which also elects a representative to serve on the Council. The Council elects a Finance and General Purposes Committee and a Training Committee and considers all recommendations put to it by these Committees and by Special Groups. It reports on its work to the Annual Conference, which is held in varying parts of the country. The Conference not only deals with the business of the Association but provides for the attendance of the leading publishers of the country to take part in joint discussions on important trade topics.

It is the Council which is the 'parliament' of booksellers and which makes most of the decisions. Some decisions, on matters of far-reaching importance, require a mandate from the membership as a whole, and such matters are referred by the Council to the Annual Conference, which is also the annual general meeting of the Association.

Perhaps it should be made clear at the outset that the Booksellers Association *has no power to fix publishers' terms*, and neither this Association nor the Publishers Association can force a publisher to agree to accept recommendations made by them. Nevertheless, both Associations exert considerable influence throughout the trade and are very active for its welfare.

The Booksellers Association is a democratic body, and opportunities are provided for any member-bookseller, however new to the trade, to air his views, and if they are sound they will be passed on to Council for action to be taken if that is necessary.

The president is the chairman of the Council, which consists of the officers and twenty-one members. The branches are East Midland, Eastern, Hampshire, Ireland, Northern Ireland, London, Midland, North-Eastern, North-Western, Oxford, Scottish, South-Western, Sussex, Western and South Wales, and Yorkshire.

Eligibility for Membership

The following firms, companies and individuals are eligible for membership of the Association:

(a) All firms, companies and individuals who carry on, in the United Kingdom and the Republic of Ireland, the work of bona-fide booksellers, and those in other parts of the world where their trade is substantially concerned with the sale of British books.

(b) Subject to recommendation of the branch, principals, directors or managers of businesses which are members of the Association and, exceptionally and by invitation of the Council, other persons in responsible positions in such businesses, and persons who have occupied any such position but who have retired from bookselling.

Membership under the second point is referred to as 'individual membership'.

Much of the detail work of the Association is carried out by committees appointed by the Council, and most members of the Council are required to serve from time to time on one or more of these. Other booksellers who are not members of the Council may also serve on certain committees.

The committees include the following:

Finance and General Purposes Committee. This, as its name implies, manages the finances of the Association as well as the other matters of importance between the Council meetings.

Training Committee. This oversees the extensive educational work of the Association, in providing training courses, organizing examinations and devising syllabuses leading to specialist certificates and the Diploma in Bookselling.

Joint Advisory Committee. This is usually referred to as the JAC and is a joint publisher-bookseller committee. Its main task is the onerous one of considering the many applications for listing in the Publishers Association's *Directory of Booksellers*, and making recommendations thereon to the Council of the Publishers Association.

In addition there are seven specialist groups (see page 138).

The Central Office

The offices referred to above are all honorary, but the work at Central Office is in the hands of a director and secretariat. One of these attends all committees, Council meetings and conferences. The secretariat, therefore, is in touch with every aspect of the trade. It prepares agenda, takes minutes and initiates action arising, issues reports, arranges conferences, prepares reports for the Press, and in general does much the same work as secretariats of similar associations, though the volume of work it handles is probably above average.

The Association also appoints representatives to serve on outside bodies where the interests of booksellers need to be watched, such as the National Book League, the *British National Bibliography*, the Retail Distributive Trades Conference, the National Chamber of Trade, and on several Publishers Association committees, dealing with book distribution, the Directory of Booksellers, the National Book Sale, the Net Book Agreement, etc.

The Branch

Every member is entitled to attend the meetings of his own branch, and has the opportunity of bringing up for discussion any issues which he feels need consideration. In a case of urgency, or if he is unable to attend a branch meeting, a member may write to the Central Office of the Association, who will advise him and, if the matter is of importance, bring it up at the first opportunity at a Council meeting. Each branch holds an annual general meeting and elects a chairman, committees, the usual other officers and elects a representative to the Council. The Council member is a most important link because he attends the Council meetings and brings to his branch a report of the discussions and decisions.

Every bookseller-member of the Association should try to keep in touch by attending branch meetings and conferences. He will find there is always something to be learned and something to be gained. If he can spare the time for other committee work and would like to take an active interest, so much the better; he will soon find useful work to do in connection with the Association.

In few trades are the members more united than in bookselling; they are surely the friendliest of rivals. Many booksellers form lifelong friendships by meeting fellow booksellers at the meetings of the Association.

Membership

It is not necessary to be a member of the Association in order to obtain books from publishers or wholesalers at trade terms, but businesses which apply to join the Association are usually listed in the Publishers Association's *Directory of Booksellers*.

A retail trader who wishes to sell books should apply on the appropriate form to the Publishers Association for listing in the Publishers Association's *Directory of Booksellers*. This application is first considered by the Joint Advisory Committee (JAC) and then goes forward, with a recommendation, to the Council of the Publishers Association for a final decision. The booksellers have a voice in the matter through their representative on the JAC.

It should be clearly understood that, however strongly a bookseller may feel that his own business is likely to be affected by a new bookshop opening in his vicinity, the listing of that new shop cannot be withheld solely on those grounds, since by law the Publishers Association cannot operate a 'distance limit'. This is, in the view of many people, rather regrettable, and there are many reasons for arguing that some area control of bookshops might prove to be in the interest not only of the booksellers but of the public and the publishers.

Membership of the Booksellers Association is quite a separate matter. Once a business has been listed, it may apply for corporate membership of the Association. After the war certain additional qualifications for membership were laid down, relating to the quantity of stock, and quality of service, but at the 1951 Conference of the Booksellers Association it was decided that these additional qualifications should no longer be insisted upon, and that membership should be open to all bona-fide booksellers. There is a provision however, that where a firm has been listed in the *Directory* for a certain category of book only, e.g. juvenile books, or books on fishing, he may join the Association only if his business is mainly that of bookselling.

It is therefore open to any bona-fide book retail business, with the one proviso mentioned above, to apply to join the Booksellers Association and enjoy the rights and privileges of membership, such as participation in the Booksellers Clearing House for accounts, the right to stock and sell book tokens, to attend and vote at general and branch meetings, to serve on committees, and to receive the bulletins.

Individual Membership

Individual membership of the Booksellers Association is open to *assistants* in the trade who have completed five years' service in bookselling and are not less than twenty-one years of age; also to assistants who hold the Booksellers' Diploma, irrespective of age. There is also a grade of membership for younger assistants, who must have spent six months in the book trade and have attained the age of sixteen years. Many young booksellers have become their firm's representative in corporate membership after being individual members and have paid tribute to the benefit derived from meeting their fellow booksellers after working hours, from listening to publishers and booksellers, and from visiting printing and binding works, and so on.

In order to seek the best opinion in matters affecting specialized aspects of bookselling, the Council of the Booksellers Association has also set up certain groups, to which members may belong. These groups meet whenever items of major importance arise in their particular field, and form a valuable medium for the interchange of information and experience among booksellers with like problems. The groups, at present, are as follows:

Library booksellers
Foreign bookselling
University and college booksellers
School Suppliers
Export
Religious Booksellers
Charter Booksellers (i.e. stockholding bookshops)

Other services provided by the Booksellers Association include:

(a) An up-to-date file of all services and supplies which are likely to be of interest to its members. Information on shop-fittings, furnishing, display units, shelving, flooring, lighting and window-dressing is available.
(b) Regular Press releases designed to draw public attention to bookshop services and interests.
(c) Members have their own bulletin, *Bookselling News*, which brings them a record of the Council's work and other information about bookselling affairs.

Everyone working in bookselling should join in the work of the Booksellers Association. The complete vindication of the Net Book Agreement was, as I said at the beginning of this chapter, a tremendous triumph, and a direct result of the working faith of booksellers in it and of their efforts to preserve it. An Association, like an army, exists to maintain peace and security; it is only when these are threatened that many appreciate the need for it. In peaceful years it is easy to regard it as an expense, a luxury, and a comparatively useless body, attempting little and achieving nothing; but the truth is that there would be little left of the trade as we know it were it not for the work of booksellers within their Association, working in close co-operation with the Publishers Association.

16

Charter Bookselling

Over several decades there emerged a pattern of thinking in bookselling and publishing. This pattern took shape because there were many people concerned about the book trade and its many problems. These people possessed a common desire to do all in their power to improve things, so it could only be a question of time before something positive was done.

Charter Bookselling with its idealistic aims was the result. The scheme was accepted and brought into being by the trade in 1964.

The principal aims of the Charter Group are to encourage the holding of a wide range of stock and the training of staff. By these means it is firmly believed that both the quality and prosperity of bookselling will be raised.

Membership of the Charter Group means that a bookseller subscribes to the basic standards of a good bookshop, and joins a Group which declares its dedication to the maintenance and improvement of these standards.

The Charter Scheme is operated as a Group under the rules of the Booksellers Association. The Group elects its own committee and officers and is free to make to the Council of the Booksellers Association such recommendations about these conditions as it considers necessary from time to time.

The vexed question of terms was one many in the trade wished to resolve but they did not see the answer simply in increased discounts, as it was thought that such, generally applied, would tend to dissipate anything extra the publishers might be able to allow, as the bad bookshop, giving relatively poor service, would benefit as much as the better bookshops. Many publishers felt they would like to support with better terms the booksellers, both large and small, who were really trying to keep to the highest standards of bookselling, especially as regards getting 'Books to Order' when not in stock, having the important Reference Books to enable them to deal with customers' queries, and having staff trained in their use and in bookselling generally.

Overall Charter Bookselling is a manifestation of the desire of the trade to improve, not only economically but idealistically. Booksellers regard their calling as one of national—indeed international—importance, so to have the best possible book-shops in every town with properly trained staff is the object and aim of the scheme.

The Charter Group operates with a number of committees—the Executive, the Publicity, the Liaison and the Obligations. It produces an annual report which incorporates 'The Results of Bookselling' for the year. This, to my mind, is the most valuable statistical survey available. It divides bookshops into categories depending on their turnover. The figures are based on confidential returns made by Charter booksellers. Charter booksellers are, under the Charter Scheme, obligated to make returns to enable this analysis to be made.

Total sales, gross profits, expenses as a percentage of sales, trading profits, number of times book stock is turned over per annum, sales per person, sales per square foot, etc., etc., are all worked out and obviously this guide enables a bookseller to see if by comparison he is doing well or not.

If the Charter Group had succeeded only in providing these figures—and here one must acknowledge the trade's indebtedness to Mr Eric Bailey (former Treasurer and a Past President of the Booksellers Association) for getting this off the ground—it would have achieved a great deal, but it has done more—much more. But, of course, it has its critics—for instance, the total of New Book Stock required to qualify for membership is ridicu-lously small—but such criticism is a healthy sign and not surprising in a trade of particularly articulate people.

One of the great problems of British bookselling is that it takes a long time to get a book that has been specially ordered by a customer—anything from three days to almost a month, with perhaps two weeks as an average from the date of posting the order to receipt of the books by the bookseller. The Charter League table gives details of the average number of days taken by publishers as recorded by a number of important booksellers in various parts of the country. This exposes the state of affairs and has kept publishers on their toes.

In the same way that the advent of Charter Bookselling undoubtedly had a great influence on booksellers obtaining better terms from the publishers, so too does the League Table stimulate publishers to expedite deliveries. This important work, which was pioneered by Mr Julian Blackwell of Oxford, is now in charge of a specially appointed officer of the Booksellers Association.

Aims of the Charter Group

1 To maintain the highest standards of bookselling.
2 To lay down minimum training requirements for management and staff, with the aim of securing more efficient and knowledgeable service in Charter Bookshops.
3 To encourage the development of well-stocked bookshops for the customer's benefit and to emphasize to publishers the importance to them of good stock-holding booksellers.
4 To give members advice and help in displaying and publicizing books.
5 To make efficient bookselling more profitable.

Qualifications

Membership of the Group entails a minimum shop space and an annual declaration of the value of the stock held by the bookseller. Specified trade bibliographies must be possessed by the bookseller, who also undertakes to order any book not in stock, whenever possible. These are the fundamental standards of a good bookshop, and these are the prerequisites of membership.

In addition the bookseller undertakes to support the training schemes of the Group, and to make returns of his trading figures available in confidence to an independent accountant for incorporation in the economic survey. According to the size of the business, an annual levy is paid by each bookseller to the Central Development Fund for the promotion of the Group's activities. A directory of Charter booksellers is published from time to time.

Achievements

The outstanding achievement of the Charter Group has been, and continues to be, in the field of training. Residential courses for the Charter Group are now offered at three levels: Basic, Middle Management and Senior Management. There is no doubt that training is becoming a more and more important part of modern careers, and that experience, the best training of all, is not enough. Although training is organized by the Booksellers Association as a whole, the Charter Group has taken particular initiative in promoting this activity.

For the first time ever, trade statistics culled from more than a representative selection of booksellers throughout the country are available from an annual economic survey which was first published in 1964. Booksellers can compare their performance with the anonymous averages shown by the survey. Before this there was no yardstick. It also shows, in irrefutable form, the trading margins necessary to make bookselling viable, and it should be taken to heart by those publishers not yet supporting the charter in tangible form.

In addition to the main Executive Committee, a number of active sub-committees meet regularly, covering such activities as Publicity, Training, and Trading Margins. A vital consideration to Charter booksellers is the modernization and improvement of their shops and fittings, and half a million was spent by Charter booksellers from the initiation of the Charter to 1966, a substantial investment which has produced dramatic increases of sales.

Future

Membership of the Charter Group means that a bookseller subscribes to the basic standards of a good bookshop and joins a Group which declares its dedication to the maintenance and improvement of those standards. This is symbolized by the Charter sign, which is proudly displayed by Charter booksellers and which the public will increasingly recognize as a measure of quality and service.

Conditions of Membership of the Charter Group of the Booksellers Association for New Applicants from 1 January 1968

1. *Constitution*

The Charter scheme is operated as a Group under the rules of the Association. The Group elects its own committee and officers and is free to make to the Council of the Association recommendations about these conditions, as it regards necessary from time to time. The Group's activities are financed by an annual levy upon its members.

2. *Membership*

(a) A firm which applies for membership of the Group for the first time should have been selling books in an established bookshop which has been a member of the Association for at least two years.

(b) If the proprietor or manager of a bookshop applying for membership for the first time has been in the book trade for ten years or holds the Association's Diploma, the firm's period of trading—from the date of its membership of the Association—may be reduced to one year.

(c) A new branch of an existing bookshop may be accepted immediately but only if the parent shop is a member of the Group and has fulfilled all its Charter obligations for the past two years.

(d) A new applicant for membership is required to complete

the declaration form and pay the first year's levy before the application is granted.

(e) Any member who fails to carry out the obligations set out in paragraphs 4 to 6 below, or who fails to maintain the minimum standards set out in paragraph 3, shall be expelled from the Group, with the right of appeal to a sub-committee of the Association's Council.

(f) A member may be readmitted to the Group on payment of his levy for the current year, on completion of a new declaration form and after confirmation from the Association's nominated accountant that a fully completed economic survey for the last full year has been submitted.

3. *Book Stock and Floor Space*

(a) The minimum book stock (excluding second-hand) is £2,000 as valued in the last annual balance sheet. The stock figure must be declared annually within eight weeks of the request coming from the Association.

(b) The minimum shop floor space is 150 sq. ft open to the public and devoted to the display and sale of new books.

(c) The minimum window display space is a window or windows of 5 ft width showing on to a public thoroughfare.

4. *Service to the Public*

(a) The bookshop must be open to the general public during the normal working week.

(b) It is the practice of the shop to obtain, whenever possible, books not in stock.

(c) The bookshop must be equipped with the minimum of any one of the following trade bibliographies:

  (i) Whitaker Service: *The Bookseller* (weekly); the *Cumulative Book List* (quarterly cumulations and annual volumes); *Whitaker's British Books in Print* (as published).

  (ii) British National Bibliography Service: Weekly and Monthly parts; Quarterly cumulations; Annual volumes; plus Whitaker's *British Books in Print* (as published).

5. Training

(a) Training obligations are calculated in units, one unit being either:

  (i) Residential Course.
  (ii) Approved correspondence course.
  (iii) Approved one-day release course (minimum three days) or approved evening course (minimum ten sessions).
  (iv) Approved in-firm training.

(b) For every two members of staff employed wholly or mainly in buying and selling new books (which normally excludes packers, typists, invoice clerks and accounts department staff), one unit of training must be undertaken in any three-year period.

NOTE: In the case of businesses with five or more full-time sales staff, half of the units of training in a three-year period for any one shop must consist of outside courses.

Businesses with less than five full-time sales staff can fulfil their obligations with approved in-firm training, although some attendance at outside courses should be undertaken where possible.

6. Group Finance and Economic Survey

(a) There is a levy of £1 per head of total staff engaged full time in bookselling operations, including proprietor and Manager, and packing and clerical staff, but excluding those engaged full time in sales of second-hand books and books not in the English language. (Part-time staff should be calculated in man-hours, each forty hours counting as one full-time staff.) This levy must be paid within eight weeks of the date of the request being sent out by the Association.

(b) A member must submit, in confidence, through his own accountant, to an independent accountant appointed by the Association, such trading figures as are agreed by the Group to be necessary for the production of a summary of the general economic trends of stockholding bookselling.

The declaration form for new applicants for membership to Charter Bookselling is given on pages 148–9.

THE CHARTER SCHEME DECLARATION FORM FOR NEW MEMBERS.

(Please read the notes "How to Take Part" before attempting to complete this Declaration)

NOTE: A Declaration form in respect of each place of business is required.

a) The book stock (excluding second-hand volumes) as valued in the last annual accounts amounts to : £——

 NOTE: The minimum new book stock requirement is £2,000

b) The shop floor space open to the public and devoted to the display and sale of new books is: —— Sq. ft.

 NOTE: The minimum requirement is 150 sq. ft.

c) The width of shop display windows to the public thoroughfare is: —— ft.

 NOTE: The minimum requirement is 5 ft.

d) The shop is open to the general public at the following times during the week:

————————   ————————

————————   ————————

————————   ————————

e) One of the following trade bibliographical services is kept in the shop in current edition. Please indicate which.

 i) Whitaker   ii) British National Bibliography   i)——
 (For details of each service, see note 4(c) in "How to Take Part")   ii)——
 It is the practice of the shop to obtain, whenever possible books not in stock.

g) Sales staff will be entered for the Association's training courses in accordance with the requirements set out in para 4(b) of "How to Take Part" (Ref: 290/71). For purposes of calculation for these courses, only the *sales* staff should be taken into account.

h) The annual Group Levy for 1971 of £1 per head of total staff engaged full-time in bookselling operations, including proprietor and manager and packing and clerical staff, but excluding those engaged full-time in sales of second-hand books and books not in the English language, is attached.

 NOTE: Part-time staff should be calculated in man-hours, each 40 hours counting as one full-time staff.

(continued)

j) Such figures as are agreed by the Group to be necessary for producing a summary of economic trends in stockholding bookselling, will be submitted in confidence to an independent accountant nominated by the Association.

k) (i) *Total* number of staff (including packers, managerial and clerical staff) engaged in new book business (part-time to be calculated on man-hour basis, 40 hours to week). ____

   (ii) Number of *sales* staff (including managerial but not clerical staff and packers). ____

Signature of *Proprietor/Director/Manager ————————————————————

Name of business ————————————————————————————

Address ———————————————————————————————————

———————————————————————————————————————

Date ———————————————

* Delete whichever is not applicable

Please complete this form and send it to:

> The Secretary,
> The Booksellers Association of Great Britain and Ireland,
> 152 Buckingham Palace Road,
> LONDON SW1W 9TZ

NOTE: If your business does not fulfil the conditions laid down, or you are unable to give the undertakings required, but you believe that there are individual circumstances which entitle you to special consideration, you may lodge an appeal to the Council of the Association.

17

Book Tokens

Book Tokens are now familiar to most people. The scheme first devised by a publisher, Mr Harold Raymond, of Chatto and Windus, London, was started in 1932 and became an immediate success; booksellers' turnover in tokens increased from £16,000 in 1935 to almost £2,000,000 in the year ending 30 April, 1972.

The book-token system is designed to stimulate the giving of books as presents; tokens permit the presentation of a book where there is uncertainty as to the literary tastes or requirements of the recipient. Tokens are easy to send through the post; no packing is required—they are posted in correspondence envelopes.

A British book token is exchangeable in almost any good bookshop in Great Britain and Ireland, and also in Holland and South Africa. Book tokens can be purchased in Holland and South Africa and exchanged in British bookshops.

Book tokens consist of a series of attractive greetings cards, on part of which is affixed by the bookseller a book-token stamp of the value required. Special stamps of 20p, 25p, 50p, £1, £2, £5, are issued, but more than one stamp may be affixed to one token card to make up varying amounts if care is taken to avoid covering the serial number which each stamp bears. Book tokens are not intended to be sold instead of books, but their purpose is to enable a bookseller to make a sale when difficulties of choice or limitation of stock would otherwise prevent it. The donor sends the book token to the recipient, and the recipient takes or posts it to the bookseller of his choice.

Most booksellers now agree that book tokens are an asset to

the trade. They remark that the exchangers of book tokens are not as fussy as other customers regarding the condition of books and more particularly of book jackets, and consequently stock which might prove a little difficult to sell in the ordinary way (as it has been too frequently handled) moves readily to customers shopping with book tokens. Obviously a person wishing to buy a book to send as a present requires a copy in mint condition, whereas the exchanger of a book token usually requires the book for personal use and, within reason, its condition is less important.

Another advantage is that the majority of book tokens are exchanged after the Christmas season and this stimulates trade at what would otherwise be a quiet period. It is also found that exchangers of book tokens often buy books to a greater value than the tokens they possess, and this represents extra business which would probably not have materialized but for the fact that the customers had tokens they wished to exchange and therefore entered the bookshop for this purpose.

Ordering and Selling Book Tokens

The company operating the scheme, Book Tokens Ltd, is owned by the Booksellers Association of Great Britain and Ireland. The directors and management are, therefore, appointed by the booksellers themselves and the whole scheme is worked for the benefit of the trade and administered by the company for the Booksellers Association.

There is a charge of 3p for each standard book-token card, and this amount is added to the price of the token stamp; therefore a 20p book token costs the purchaser 23p and a £1 token, £1.03. There are also larger cards which cost 5p. This charge of 3p or 5p for each token-card—the service fee—is to cover manufacturing costs and tax; the income pays for the running of the token scheme, and it is handed over in full to Book Tokens Ltd.

The profit on the sale of a book by means of a token is shared by the bookseller who originally sold the token, and the exchanging bookseller. This is how it is arranged. The stamps are issued from Book Tokens Ltd, on application from a bookseller (the form is shown on pages 160–1). The bookseller is not charged for them until they have been sold, but he is requested to fill in the form quarterly, giving details of the unsold stamps in hand, and he is allowed a discount of 12½ per cent off the face value of the stamps sold. On this form he also gives particulars of the total of each value stamp he has exchanged for books, and all these cancelled tokens have to be returned with the form. The bookseller receives the face value of the stamps exchanged less 12½ per cent. Thus the seller and the exchanger share equally the profits of the transaction. At the time of settlement the bookseller also pays for all token cards sold by him. It will therefore be seen that the company acts as a clearing house for booksellers' token transactions.

Miscellaneous Points about Tokens

Can book tokens be credited to a customer's account? The short answer is 'No', but it is more accurate to say: 'Not for the purpose of paying for books purchased in the past and never for any commodity other than books'. Most booksellers will accept tokens from customers who cannot immediately decide upon their requirements, and record them in a thumb-index book under the customer's name. The usual entry gives the name and address of the customer, the value of the tokens deposited, the number of each token stamp, the value of the books taken and the date. In this way the bookseller has a record of the transaction without making any entries in his accounts. It is advisable for booksellers to refuse to enter small balances. It is best to suggest to customers a paperback or some other cheap book, pointing out that, according to regulations, tokens should be exchanged for books to the 'full value' at the time of the exchange.

Book tokens can be accepted by booksellers who are not members of the Booksellers Association, for instance certain dealers in second-hand books. In this case, however, a charge of 3p for each exchange is made by Book Tokens Ltd.

The right to stock and sell Book Tokens is confined to members of the Booksellers Association of Great Britain and Ireland. To administer the working of the scheme a Limited Company was set up, the Directors of which are appointed by the Council of the Association. These Directors, who give their service voluntarily, meet regularly throughout the year to deal with the routine business of the Company. They report to the Council and invite its guidance where matters of policy are involved.

Book Tokens Ltd hope and expect members to use their best endeavours to promote the sale and exchange of Book Tokens to the benefit of the public and the book trade alike.

Any member wishing to raise a point in connection with the working of the scheme can do so by writing direct to the Secretary of the Company at 152 Buckingham Palace Road, London SW1W 9TZ, or alternatively through his local Branch or through his Branch representative on the Council. The Board of Book Tokens Ltd is always glad to receive and consider suggestions or criticisms from members of the Association, for whose benefit the scheme is run.

Rules and Instructions

Definition of the Scheme

The Book Token Scheme is a scheme whereby members of the public can purchase from a bookseller (the issuing bookseller) Tokens which will be accepted by him or by any other bookseller (the exchanging bookseller) as valid in exchange for books to the full value of the amount indicated by a stamp or stamps on the Token Card.

1. A Scheme for Members only

Only booksellers who are Members of the Booksellers Association of Great Britain and Ireland are eligible to participate in the Scheme; but the Company reserves the right to refuse Tokens to any bookseller without giving any reason for such refusal and irrespective of his eligibility for participation in the scheme by virtue of membership of the Booksellers Association of Great Britain and Ireland or otherwise. In order to be regarded as a participator a member must agree to sell and exchange Tokens throughout the year.

2. Orders for Token Cards

Token Cards issued by Book Tokens Ltd (hereinafter called 'the Company') are sold firm to booksellers. The Company may at any time alter the terms or price at which Token Cards are sold to booksellers.

Booksellers are asked to order Token Cards in multiples of ten. Minimum post free order forty cards. With small orders 5p postage must be remitted.

3. Net Price of Token Card

The bookseller must charge such price as may be laid down from time to time by the Company for each Token Card sold. Failure to do so will disqualify the bookseller from participation in the Book Token Scheme (see also Rule 11).

4. Value of Token Stamps

Token Stamps are supplied in denominations of 20p, 25p, 50p, £1, £2, £5, or such other values as may from time to time be agreed upon by the Company.

5. Method of issue

The issuing bookseller must fill in particulars on the Token Card and affix the stamp in accordance with the following instructions:

The name and address of the issuing bookseller must be printed, written or stamped in the space indicated on the Token Card. The Token Stamp affixed by the issuing bookseller must not be marked in any way by him. More than one stamp may be affixed to one Token Card to make up a composite price, but care should be used to leave the serial numbers clearly visible. It is not sufficient to pin or clip the stamps on the card.

6. Stamps On Sale or Return

Token Stamps are supplied on sale or return to booksellers whose application to open an account has been approved by the Company. In all other cases they are supplied for cash. Stamps on sale or return remain the property of the Company and must be paid for if lost.[1] The right to receive stamps on sale or return may be withdrawn if, in the opinion of the Directors of the Company, the bookseller's transactions become unsatisfactory; he will then be supplied with stamps only for cash less the discount ruling at the date of purchase. The Directors may at their discretion authorize the recall, collection or inspection of stocks of Token Stamps already supplied on sale or return, and it is a condition of the supply of Token Stamps on sale or return that the bookseller must permit the authorized representative of the Company to inspect or collect stocks of Token Stamps at any time during business hours on being given reasonable notice of his intention to do so.

It is in the common interest that Token Stamps should be placed in the charge of a responsible person and kept in a secure place, and the serial numbers recorded on receipt of stamps from the Company. All stamps and books of stamps should be sold in strictly numerical order. It is recommended that Book Token Stamps be insured against loss by fire or theft and that proper records be kept of transactions so that any such loss can be accurately substantiated (see footnote).

7. Cancellation of Exchanged Stamps

Tokens presented for exchange must be cancelled by the exchanging bookseller immediately they are received.

The exchanging bookseller must write or stamp his name and address across the Token Stamps in such a manner as not to obliterate the serial numbers.

As a protection against theft Book Tokens which do not bear the issuing bookseller's name should not be exchanged without reference to the Company.

---

[1] Booksellers would be well advised to ensure that they are adequately covered for the value of the exchanged Book Tokens they hold, as well as the value of unissued Book Tokens. If lost the insurers could argue that these are not stock or cash and are not, therefore, covered by insurance unless specially covered.

In his own interests a bookseller should beware of accepting large numbers of Tokens from unknown persons without verification by the Company.

8. Validity of Exchange

There is now no time limit on the validity of Book Tokens. This rule applies to all Tokens, although some cards refer to a period of validity of twelve months or two years.

9. Lost Tokens

Tokens lost by members of the public may be replaced only at the discretion of the Company. No claims for such replacements will be entertained until twelve months have elapsed from the time the loss is reported to the Company. No claim for replacement can be considered unless the serial numbers of the lost tokens are known.

10. Official Token Cards Only

Token Stamps must be used only on the Token Cards issued by the Company. Stamps only, or stamps affixed to any other description of card or paper, are not valid for exchange.

N.B. Any breach of this rule will involve the selling bookseller in a special fee of 15p for every Token so presented for credit.

11. Book Tokens used as School Prizes

When Book Tokens are bought by Schools for use as prizes, and a certificate is obtained from the Headmaster or his accredited representative to the effect that they will be so used, Token Cards may, as a concession, be sold at ½p each, or such concessionary price as the Company may from time to time determine. Booksellers will be credited with the difference in price of cards so supplied on production of the certificate referred to above.

12. Exchangeable only for Books

Tokens are exchangeable only for books. They may not be exchanged for wholly or partly other goods, or for cash or for a library subscription or for subscriptions to periodicals. If the bookseller wishes, he may accept Tokens in exchange for second-hand books.

If a customer wishes to hand in Book Tokens without at that time ordering specific books, the value of the Token should not be credited to the customer's account. A special register of such Book Tokens should be kept against which subsequent purchases may be placed, or a Credit Note, exchangeable for books only, may be issued to the customer.

13. *Accounts*

Booksellers shall account to the Company for sales and exchanges of Tokens in such form and at such periods as shall from time to time be prescribed by the Company. Booksellers who fail to render their accounts within seven days after the second application shall be liable to be regarded as unsatisfactory in their transactions (see Rule 6).

The Summary and Statement of Account (Form 'A') is normally made up four times a year at the following dates: 31 January, 30 April, 31 July, 31 October. The bookseller must complete the Form 'A' in accordance with the instructions thereon and return it without delay to the Company. At each accounting details of stock must be recorded in the space provided, even though no sales have been made during that period. Letters, etc., giving particulars of sales and/or exchanges are not sufficient. Only signed copies of the official form 'A' will be accepted. Additional copies of Form 'A' may be had on application to the Company.

14. *Remittance of Cash Differences*

Where the net value of the Tokens sold plus charges for cards, etc., exceeds the net value of the Tokens exchanged the difference is due to the Company and the remittance must be sent with the account. Where the net value of Tokens exchanged exceeds that of Tokens sold plus net charges the Company will issue a cheque to the bookseller.

15. *Extra Charges*

Booksellers who are not participants in the Company's scheme will be charged a fee of 3p for every Stamp when claiming settlement. Such settlement will also be subject to a deduction of the discount due to the issuing bookseller. This shall apply both to members and non-members of the Booksellers Association of Great Britain and Ireland. The exchanging bookseller is not permitted to deduct from the value of the Token any sum by way of compensation for the issuing bookseller's share of discount remitted to the Company or for any other reason whatsoever. Customers are entitled to receive a book or books to the full face value of the Token.

16. *Return of Stamps where a Business changes hands*

Where a bookselling business ceases to exist or changes hands or goes into liquidation or on the occasion of the death of the proprietor all unsold stocks of Token Stamps must be returned to the Company if they are held on sale or return. Fresh stocks will not be issued to the successor(s) until confirmation has been obtained from the Booksellers Association of Great Britain and Ireland that transfer of membership has been granted.

17. *Private Gift Voucher Schemes*

Any firm operating a private voucher scheme may also participate in the scheme operated by Book Tokens Ltd, subject to their co-operation as follows:

(a) The word 'token' shall not be used in connection with the operation of any private schemes, nor appear in the advertising material or publicity connected therewith.

(b) The design of the voucher or receipt used in such scheme, and wording thereon, shall not be a colourable imitation of the general design and wording of the cards issued by Book Tokens Ltd.

18. *Interpretation of These Rules*

All persons or companies selling or exchanging Book Tokens agree to do so in accordance with the foregoing rules 1–17 and the explanatory notes subjoined, and in the event of any dispute to accept the Directors' decision as final.

If a bookseller has any difficulty regarding the scheme he is advised to consult his Branch Secretary or Representative Member of the Council of the Booksellers Association of Great Britain and Ireland.

The Summary and Statement of Account (Form 'A') referred to on page 157 is reproduced on pages 160–1.

BOOK TOKENS
SUMMARY AND STATEMENT

Form

A

No.....................................

Messrs.....................................

Address.....................................

Cr. **Tokens Exchanged**
Tokens exchanged can be credited only if the cancelled stamps accompany this summary.

	No. Ex'd.	Value		£	p
A. OLD Series Stamps		3/6	17½p		
		5/–	25p		
E.B.O.		7/6	37½p		
		10/6	52½p		
		12/6	62½p		
		15/–	75p		
		21/–	£1.05		
		105/–	£5.25		
		Gross Total			
		Less 12½%			
		Net Total, Old Series			

	No. Ex'd.	Value			
B. NEW Series Stamps		4/–	20p		
		5/–	25p		
E.B.N.		10/–	50p		
		£1			
		£2			
		£5			
		Gross Total			
		Less 12½%			
		Net Total, New Series			
		Grand Net Total, All Exchanges			

To **Book Tokens Limited,**
152 Buckingham Palace Road, London, SW1W 9TZ

Please send / We enclose remittance of **£** : being the difference between Tokens taken in exchange, as claimed above (cancelled stamps for which are attached), and the net value of Tokens sold (plus net charges if any) as shown opposite.

Signature.....................................
Please return the top copy to B.T. Ltd. with as little delay

LIMITED

OF ACCOUNT.................................

....

....

	B. T. Ltd
	Ledger
	Folio

....

Dr. **Tokens Sold** BOOK TOKENS LIMITED renders Statement of Account herewith. Please deduct stock in hand from Total of Tokens O/S. The difference represents value of Tokens sold.

Date	Goods Supplied	Invoice No.	O/S (Subject 12½%)		★ Net Charges	
....	Stock in hand at previous A/C		....	....	....	....
....						
....						
....						
....						
....						
....						
....						
....						

STOCK IN HAND
Please enter complete details below

Number	Value	£	P
....	20p		
....	25p		
....	50p		
....	£1		
....	£2		
....	£5		

Total (to be deducted from Total O/S)

Less 12½%

★ Add Net Charges

NET TOTAL

★ Token Cards etc. not already paid for

as possible and retain the carbon copy for your own file.

18

Booksellers Clearing House

The Booksellers Clearing House was set up in 1948 by the Booksellers Association after consultation with the Publishers Association. The Scheme is managed by the Association's Book Tokens Limited. This scheme enables a bookseller to pay the majority of his monthly accounts from publishers by means of one cheque. He completes a printed form, which sets out the names of some 300 publishers and other suppliers to the book trade, by filling in against each name the amount he wishes to pay. The bookseller draws one cheque for the total made payable to the Booksellers Clearing House and sends the form, the cheque and all the individual publishers' statements to BCH. On receipt of the bookseller's payment instructions and cheque, the Clearing House sorts the statements into publisher order and then draws one cheque for each publisher which is dispatched together with the relevant statements and a machine list showing how the total is calculated. The advantages to the bookseller are obvious, for it saves him the task of preparing individual cheques and envelopes and, of course, it saves both postage and time. It is also to the publishers' advantage for booksellers to pay through this system, for any scheme which simplifies settlement and helps a bookseller keep to a timetable must encourage prompt payment.

There are no fees payable by either the bookseller or the publisher involved.

Booksellers must make their remittances to BCH on or before the 21st of each month and in its turn BCH pays publishers on or before the 28th of each month.

For publishers to participate there is no need for any change in their accounting procedure but BCH do ask that tear-off remittance advices (which are often substituted for statements) should be of reasonable substance and size to bear both the publisher's name and the bookseller's name so as to avoid loss or mistakes when handling the vast numbers of statements and remittance advices which pass through the Clearing House each month. Full details of this scheme are obtainable from The Booksellers Clearing House, 152 Buckingham Palace Road, London SW1W 9TZ.

19

The National Book Sale

The National Book Sale has become an important 'event' in the bookselling year and one valuable to the book-buying public and bookseller alike. The first Sale was held in February 1955 and it is now held annually.

Britain's National Book Sale is unique in that it is so designed that all participants hold the sale at the same time throughout the country. This is the strength of the sale as it inspires the confidence of the shopping public in its genuineness and permits advertising on a national scale.

Like any other sale in retailing, the National Book Sale presents an opportunity for a bookseller to dispose of his old and surplus stock and to 'buy in' for the sale bargains from the manufacturers—in this case publishers' overstocks. By special arrangement, publishers usually only charge one quarter of the published price for books they offer for the sale and booksellers offer these bargains to their customers at half the published price and if any stock remains these excellent 'terms' permit booksellers to sell off during the last two days of the sale any remaining sale stock at cost or even less and still on average make a good profit.

A number of booksellers still do not take part in the sale and controversy still occurs on certain points regarding it. These points come up year after year at Booksellers' Conferences and there have been experiments as regards the dates for the sale and the length of the sale. It is obviously difficult to please everybody and whatever dates are selected they present certain difficulties for some. Originally the sales were held near the end of January in each year, but this was found to be inconvenient, as publishers had to give attention to sales overstocks at a time when they were full-out dealing with Christmas orders. The same, of course, applied to booksellers and the latter were further inconvenienced by the arrival of sale stock when they were grappling with either the Christmas trade or stocktaking, as many businesses take stock at the end of January.

Other dates conflicted either with university bookselling's busy period or school trade or, in seaside areas, peak holiday periods. The sale, it is felt, must be linked within reasonable time with the sale periods of retailing generally, i.e. July or January, as the public is more sales-conscious at these times.

As regards length of the sale there is no doubt that in London a crisp, short sale achieves the best results, but outside large cities and towns a longer sale may have advantages. A time-limit must be fixed and the whole sale properly controlled and organized as during the sale period the Net Book Agreement is relaxed for licensed participating booksellers.

I have the honour of being regarded as the Father of Britain's National Book Sale as it was largely due to my interest and persistence that, after many years of opposition, an experimental sale was tried. Britain's National Book Sales are acknowledged to be successful but in my view they could be more so if:

1. Every bookseller in the country, including the large multiple bookshops, tried to ensure that he had a successful sale at the agreed sale period.
2. Publishers sold their overstocks to booksellers only, not to remainders-men. One of the original objects of the sale was to channel more publishers' remainders through the bookshops.
3. Booksellers kept strictly to the 'Rules' which the National Book Sale committee issue—particularly regarding the duration of the sale—as these are worked out to be in the best interests of all concerned.

Sales are valuable as they bring into the bookshops customers who otherwise would not be there. Once there, they may buy sale bargains or books at full price, or they may see books they like and return time and time again to buy more. Sales are valuable, too, as they create goodwill—everyone likes a bargain—and by clearing old stock room is made for newer books which will sell more readily. In view of all these advantages a bookseller who does not participate in the sale must be missing opportunity.

Booksellers participating in the National Book Sale must apply for a Licence annually. There is a small fee for this Licence to provide a fund which is spent on publicity material, which is then supplied 'free' to licensed booksellers and for press and other advertising.

The Conditions of the Sale are constantly reviewed by The National Book Sale committee, which is a joint committee of the Publishers Association with representatives from both the Booksellers Association and the Publishers Association. Any member of the Association, as well as the committee, is entitled to propose alteration in the usual constitutional manner and in practice the Sale committee takes careful note of the views expressed on the Sale at the Booksellers' Annual Conference, when a full report of the last Sale is given and commented on from the House.

National Book Sale

To take part in the National Book Sale you must apply on this form for a licence, which will enable you to clear your overstocks in accordance with the conditions set out below, and which will record your name on the mailing lists used by publishers to announce the availability for the sale of their own overstocks. The Licence Fee is £2 and the revenue from the fee will be devoted to publicity for the National Book Sale. *Please deal with this application at once.*

Please fill in and return the whole of this form to:

The Publishers Association, 19 Bedford Square, London WC1B 3HJ.

I ....(name)................................ (firm) of .... (address) hereby apply for a licence to take part in the National Book Sale from (dates of Sale Period), as a Retail Bookseller/Wholesale Bookseller* on the conditions set out below, which I have read and understood, and agree strictly to observe. I enclose remittance for £2. *Cheques should be made payable to "The Publishers Association".* (Note: if application is made later than (date), a late fee of £2.50 will be payable.)

Date ....Signed.......................................

* Delete which is inapplicable.

Important Note
This application must be received by (date), if your name is to appear on publishers' mailing lists. This form will be returned to you endorsed with the licence. It will also act as a receipt for the fee unless a separate receipt is demanded. It is essential that you also fill in the portion below, in block capitals.

> **Licence**

Conditions to be Observed by all Participating Publishers, Wholesalers and Retail Booksellers

1. The Sale shall not begin before .... (date), nor end after ....(date), both dates inclusive. This period is referred to in the following conditions as the Sale Period.

Booksellers' Overstocks

2. Subject to the right of a publisher to exclude his list from the Sale (see condition 3) licensed *Retail Booksellers* shall be permitted, during the Sale Period to offer at ANY PRICE NOT EXCEEDING TWO-THIRDS of the published price (i.e. at a discount of 33⅓ per cent or more off published price) any title of which they have not ordered a copy during the last twelve months. On conclusion of the Sale such books shall revert to published price *unless reduced in accordance with provisions of Clause (ii) of the Standard Conditions of Sale of Net Books.*

3. Any publisher shall have the right to stipulate that all his titles shall be excluded from the Sale, except where they have been reduced in price in accordance with the provisions of Clause (ii) of the Standard Conditions of Sale of Net Books; but no publisher shall exclude selected titles only.

National Book Sale

Name of Firm ....

Full Address ....

....

Publishers' Overstocks

4. *Publishers* taking part shall circulate as soon as possible, and in any case not later than (date), to licensed booksellers only, lists of any overstocks they wish to offer for disposal during the Sale.

5. *Publishers'* overstocks shall be offered on the following terms:— at 50 per cent off the Sale price, the Sale Price being fixed by the publisher. Sale prices shall not be more than half the published price. Not less than three copies may be ordered of books of a sale price of 50p. or less.

6. During the last two days of the Sale it shall be permissible for a *licensed bookseller* to fix his own price on such publishers' overstocks as may still be in his possession, provided always that no announcement of any kind of reduction in the Sale price is made by the bookseller prior to those days.

7. Publishers' overstocks bought by *booksellers* for disposal during the Sale but which have not been sold shall revert to full published price on conclusion of the Sale until they are remaindered by the publishers (see condition 9 below) or, alternatively, reduced in accordance with the provisions of Clause (ii) of the Standard Conditions of Sale of Net Books. *Booksellers* shall be permitted to dispose of such stocks in any subsequent officially recognised national sale at any price without reference to the publishers of the books in question.

8. Titles offered by a *publisher* at a reduced price for the Sale Period shall not within six months of the end of the Sale Period be remaindered or issued by him at a price lower than that obtaining immediately before the Sale.

9. *Booksellers* taking part shall not accept at a reduced price for the Sale the publications of a non-participating publisher unless such publications have been remaindered in accordance with trade regulations.

10. Reduction in price for the Sale Period shall not entitle booksellers to claim allowances.

11. Wholesale Booksellers taking part shall be permitted to handle publishers' overstocks subject to their agreeing terms of business with the publishers and to their supplying booksellers on the same terms and conditions, as set out above, as do publishers.

Wholesale Booksellers' Overstocks

12. Wholesale Booksellers taking part shall be permitted to offer to participating booksellers, for the period of the Sale only:—
   a) any title in their stocks, of which no copy has been ordered or otherwise added to their stock during the previous twelve months and which has not been excluded from the Sale by the publishers thereof (see condition 3), and
   b) any title in their stock, which is being offered as an overstock by the publishers thereof to licensed booksellers for the Sale Period.

13. Wholesale Booksellers shall themselves determine the discounts at which their overstocks shall be offered to licensed booksellers, but the Sale price, which shall be fixed by the wholesaler, shall not be more than half the published price. Conditions 6 and 7 above shall apply also to wholesale booksellers' overstocks supplied to booksellers for the Sale Period.

14. *General.* Books offered at Sale bargain prices shall not be offered at such prices by advertisement or otherwise more than twenty-one days before the Sale.

20

The Publishers Association

The Association, known in the book trade as the 'PA', was founded in 1896 to maintain the prices of net books. While this remains an important activity (the Association successfully defended the Net Book Agreement in the Restrictive Practices Court in 1962 and again under the Resale Prices Act in 1967) the work of the Association has been extended to serve publishers' interests in all fields of common concern.

Members of the Association are advised on all manner of technical, legal and economic aspects of publishing with a special emphasis on domestic and international copyright, including, in particular, the problem of photocopying. The PA also represents publishers in relations with the Government, local authorities and other public bodies. Examples of the Association's successful activities in these fields over the years include the relief obtained for publishers of books from Purchase Tax, Selective Employment Tax and Value Added Tax.

Contact with publishers abroad is maintained by direct relations with overseas publishers' associations as well as through the Association's membership of the International Publishers Association in which it takes an active interest. There are also important links with other trade and professional bodies concerned with the production and distribution of books, notably the Booksellers Association, the Society of Authors, the Library Association, the British Federation of Master Printers and the National Book League, as well as with the Arts Council. Close co-operation with these bodies has led to the organization of National Book

Weeks as well as the sympathetic reception of the Public Lending Right by HM Government.

Membership

Membership of the Association is open to any publisher in the UK whose business, or an appreciable part of whose business, is the publishing of books. Full membership is open to all who have carried on the business of book publishing for more than one year; associate membership is available to companies who have been in business for less than one year, or whose turnover in books is small. All members of the Association are required to undertake to maintain the Net Book Agreement and the British Publishers' Traditional Market Agreement (this is explained on page 173).

Some 380 publishers are in membership of the Association. They include the largest and most famous of British publishing houses, as well as a comprehensive range of publishing interests of all kinds. PA members account for about 95 per cent of the total publishing turnover in the UK. Subscriptions to the Association are based on the total turnover of member companies. Each member of the Association regardless of the size of its subscription, is entitled to one vote at all elections or at meetings where a vote is taken.

Organization

The Association is administered by a Council of three elected Officers (President, Vice-President and Treasurer) and twelve other members. The Officers are elected for a two-year term; one-third of the Council is elected annually for a period of three years. The executive powers of the Association lie with the fourth Officer, the Secretary, who is supported by a secretariat some forty strong. Two semi-autonomous units within the PA are the export division of the Association (the Book Development Council) and the Educational Publishers' Council. There are also specialized Groups.

A number of committees exist to investigate subjects of importance to the membership, varying from royalty and other agreements to libel, and including such annual events as the National Book Sale.

The Book Development Council

To promote British books overseas, the export department of the Association was merged with the Book Development Council Ltd in 1970 to form the PA's export division, the Book Development Council. This is administered by a Council (including *ex officio* the Vice-President and Treasurer of the PA) appointed by the PA Council but under the independent chairmanship of Sir Eric Roll. The Director and his staff give advice on export problems and maintain a credit advisory service as well as organizing the participation of British publishers in overseas exhibitions and arranging publishers' missions to foreign countries. BDC's extensive mailing lists, containing the addresses and interests of the staff of centres of higher education throughout the world, have now been merged with the UK lists of University Mailing Services and are marketed for the Association of International Book Information Services (IBIS).

The Educational Publishers Council (EPC)

The Educational Publishers Council, as the educational division of the PA, is concerned with school-books up to Sixth Form and Colleges of Education, within the United Kingdom. The Director of EPC is responsible to an elected Executive Committee of twelve members and three Officers. The function of EPC is to control policy and activities concerning schoolbook publishing in the United Kingdom. Its members' interest in the promotion of British schoolbooks overseas is served by the Schoolbook Committee of BDC, on which members of EPC serve. The membership of EPC consists of about 100 firms and is open to any member of the Association with an active and long-term interest in schoolbook publishing.

Other Specialist Groups

The Association incorporates a number of other groups concerned with specific fields of publishing. These groups were set up to facilitate a closer examination of the problems shared by members because of the kinds of books which they publish. They each operate under an Executive Committee and elect their own Officers and are served by one of the Assistant Secretaries and his staff. They are concerned with the promotion of particular categories of books by such means as exhibitions. The Children's Book Group, for instance, arranges the annual Children's Book Show. Other Groups are the Book Clubs Group, the General Books Group, the Map Group, the Medical Group, the Paperback Books Group, the Religious Book Publishers Group, and the Technical and Scientific Group. The most recent addition was the Humanities and Social Sciences Group which, with the Medical Group and Technical and Scientific Group, will be co-ordinated by a new University, College and Professional Publishing Group, which will be concerned with common problems in publishing.

Net Book Agreement

The Net Book Agreement is an undertaking signed by all members of the Association by which they agree to sell to booksellers such of their publications as they choose to issue at net prices on the strict condition that they may not be offered to the public at less than the price fixed by the publisher. Under licence from the PA booksellers may supply public libraries at a 10 per cent discount, and there are other provisions permitting the giving of discounts under licence as, for example, to those who sell religious books in church porchways, or recreational paperbacks in schools.

In vindicating the Agreement as 'not contrary to the public interest' in 1962, the Restrictive Practices Court said that without the Agreement there would be fewer stockholding booksellers, fewer books and higher prices. Since bookshops still represent the best way for publishers to maximize the sale of the vast majority of the books they publish, the administration of the Net Book Agreement remains one of the Publishers Association's prime functions.

Home Trade Services

The Association maintains directories of home and export

booksellers, and also wholesalers. Its Directory of Booksellers is the most comprehensive list of book retailers available, being supplemented each month by additions recommended by a joint committee which includes representatives of the Booksellers Association. The Association's Trade Department is responsible for maintaining the directories, as well as for issuing Library Licences and other concessions permitted under the Net Book Agreement.

The Publishers Association also operates a home credit advisory service.

The Export Market

Exports have always been an important part of British publishers' turnover, and never more so than since World War II. Today they bring in some 45 per cent of the British Book trade's total turnover. When, with the partition of India in 1947, it became apparent that the old 'empire market' was liable to disintegrate, the PA created what is now known as the British Publishers' Traditional Market Agreement. Under this Agreement member firms undertake not to accept a book for publication unless they can secure exclusive publishing rights in the English language for the British Commonwealth and Empire as it was constituted on 1 January 1947. Nowadays a different form of words is used, but the object is to retain for British publishers those markets which their enterprise and imagination developed and which their commercial skills secured. The market has been held intact, thanks to British publishers' resolute support of the Market Agreement.

Training

The staff of the Association includes a Training Development Officer, who liaises with the Printing and Publishing Industry Training Board to keep them informed of training development in the book publishing industry, and who also advises members of the Board's activities and recommendations. A number of courses and seminars are organized by the Training Department to provide unified instruction to employees of member firms at levels ranging from the elementary courses for new entrants to courses for higher management. The courses offered include editing, sub-editing, sales management and management finance, among a range of other specializations.

Industrial Relations

The Industrial Relations Unit of the Association has the services of a full-time Industrial Relations Officer to watch publishers' interests and to advise on policy and practice, and to negotiate in appropriate circumstances.

PA Publications

The Association publishes a number of booklets useful to publishers, dealing with such things as the rationalization of book production, particular aspects of copyright, market reports, and the like. A list is available on request.

One of the most important PA publications is its *Guide to Royalty Agreements*, which is available to members at a preferential price. This analyses the normal publisher's contract, clause by clause, with a commentary dealing with particular situations. Appendixes include specimen contracts for educational and technical works, the sale and purchase of translation rights, the sale of sheets, a micro-form edition licence, and a standard form of quit-claim for use with film companies.

Apart from the regular weekly issue of information circulars the Association issues a monthly Members' Circular and BDC an Export News. These printed circulars are indexed at the end of the year and are available in bound volumes.

Press Relations

The Association keeps in touch with the general and literary press for the promotion of books (in general) and the book trade including the administration, in association with the National Book League, of the annual £5,000 Booker Prize for Fiction sponsored by Booker, McConnell Ltd and the Association.

The Future

The Association has developed its activities since 1896 expressly to meet the changing needs of its membership. It is charged to keep abreast of innovations in legislation and technology and constantly to safeguard members' interests by whatsoever means it can; it is also responsible for the promotion of the welfare and prosperity of all concerned in publishing. The best and most experienced minds in publishing readily make their expertise available to the Association for the benefit of members generally. A trade association can only be as useful as its members wish and make possible; the PA is fortunate in its members.

21

The Library Licence System

Booksellers who are for the first time trying to develop trade with local librarians may find the regulations of the Library Licence a little confusing; so here is an explanation of these regulations.

The system (initially based on the Library Agreement, which came into force on 12 November 1929) was revised in 1964. The main change under the 1964 revision is that licences are issued to booksellers. Under the original system they were issued to libraries. The effect of the arrangement is to recognize, subject to certain conditions, public libraries and any other libraries which grant to the public access free of charge and which give certain public facilities for the use of books, as entitled to purchase net books at a discount from suppliers named by them.

The Issue of Licences

Since the giving of this commission involves a relaxation of the Net Book Agreement, every library that is entitled to this discount applies for a licence from the Publishers Association.

When a library licence has been granted, the name(s) of the bookseller or booksellers from whom the librarian wishes to obtain his supplies are endorsed on the licence, and a notification of the licence is sent to each bookseller named. This facsimile is the bookseller's authority to allow the discount to that library. It does not authorize him to give discount to any other library, *nor can the library itself obtain a discount from any bookseller except those named on its licence.* A facsimile of each licence is sent to the library concerned.

The Procedure for Booksellers

If a bookseller wishes to be licensed to supply a particular library, the librarian concerned must submit the bookseller's name to the Publishers Association, who will notify the Joint Advisory Committee. When the addition has been made the bookseller's licence will be appropriately endorsed, and he may then allow the discount. Many booksellers who are licensed to supply one particular library write to head office asking if they may give discounts to other libraries. As explained earlier, they cannot do this. In the same way, an institutional librarian who has heard of the licensing arrangement may tell his bookseller that other libraries are getting 10 per cent discount and claim that he should also. *The bookseller must refuse to give this discount.* The discount can be given to a library by a bookseller *only when he holds a specific licence for that library, naming him as the licensed supplier.*

A bookseller may, of course, supply any library with second-hand or non-net books, at any price he pleases, without such a licence. But where new net books are supplied by British publishers on the Standard Conditions of Sale of Net Books (as set out in the Net Book Agreement), *only a licensed library may be given a discount,* and then *only by booksellers whose names have been entered on that particular library's licence by the Publishers Association.*

Books imported from overseas publishers (whether direct or through a wholesaler) are not covered by the Library Licence Agreement, and the bookseller is not obliged to give the agreed discount on these. Care should be taken by the bookseller, however, to see if the publisher markets such books through an agent or associated company in this country, with the power to maintain a published price and authorize a discount on it. In such cases, where the agent is a signatory of the Net Book Agreement, the library discount scheme would apply.

The discount on net books may be up to 10 per cent. In practice the maximum is expected by the library authorities, but booksellers should note that where his own trade terms on a particular book are less than 16⅔ per cent plus 5 per cent the full net price should be charged. It should also be noted that the library receives its preferential treatment in consideration, *inter alia*, of prompt and regular payment of its accounts. If the library does not keep to its own part of the bargain, the bookseller should notify his Association, who, as party to the Agreement, will refer the matter, where justified, to the Publishers Association.

Although the granting of licences applies mainly to public libraries, the conditions also apply to libraries which 'grant public access', and in consequence, therefore, licences have in the past been granted to certain college and other institutional libraries which have satisfied the Publishers Association that their facilities are available for public use. Members of the Booksellers Association who wish to know whether or not particular libraries have a licence may find out through the Association.

The text of the terms and conditions governing the Library Licence and the form of Application are reproduced on pages 179–80.

THE PUBLISHERS ASSOCIATION

Net Book Agreement, 1957 (M. and N.M.)

Authorization of Grant to Libraries
of Discount on Net Books

LIBRARY LICENCE

Terms and Conditions

This Licence is issued by authority of the Council of the Publishers Association in accordance with Condition (iv) of the Standard Conditions of Sale of Net Books set out in the Net Book Agreement, 1957, to permit the Bookseller named overleaf ("the Bookseller") to supply the Library named overleaf ("the Library") with net books, solely for the use of the library but not for resale, at a discount not exceeding ten per cent. of their net published prices, subject to the following conditions:

1. Discount on net books may be allowed only in return for prompt settlement of invoices.

2. Discount may not be allowed on net books on which the Bookseller receives a discount of less than sixteen and two-thirds per cent plus five per cent.

3. Discount may be allowed only so long as the Library's total annual purchase of net books solely for the use of the library is not less than £100.

4. No consideration in cash or in kind, other than the granting of a discount permitted under this Licence, shall be offered or given by the Bookseller or sought or accepted by the Library in respect of or in connection with the supply of net books by the Bookseller to the Library.

5. Without prejudice to the generality of the last foregoing Condition, supplementary services (such as card-indexing, stamping, reinforcement of binding, the supply and fitting of plastic jackets etc.), if provided by or on behalf of the Bookseller to the Library, shall be charged and paid for at not less than the actual cost thereof to the Bookseller.

6. Books purchased under this Licence shall be purchased solely for the use of the Library and not for resale.

7. This Licence is revocable by the Council of the Publishers Association at any time but, unless revoked on account of a breach of the Standard Conditions of Sale referred to above, not less than three months previous notice shall be given.

Any breach of these terms and conditions constitutes a breach of the Standard Conditions of Sale of Net Books referred to above and will render this Licence liable to immediate revocation.

Issued by:
The Publishers Association
19 Bedford Square, London WC1B 3HJ

R. E. BARKER
Secretary.
For and on behalf of the Council

APPLICATION

To be sent to:

The Secretary
The Publishers Association
19 Bedford Square
London, W.C.1

Application is hereby made on behalf of the library named below for the bookseller(s) named below (whose willingness to supply has been ascertained) to be licensed to supply the said library with net books solely for the use of the library (but not for resale) at a discount not exceeding ten per cent. of their net published prices in accordance with the terms and conditions of the Library Licence set out overleaf.

The following undertakings are given on behalf of the applicant(s):

1. That current total annual expenditure on new net books for use in the Library is not less than £100 and that future annual expenditure on such books is expected to be about £...............*

2. That in support of the foregoing, the Library will on request provide the Publishers Association in confidence with particulars of the Library's annual expenditure on such books.

3. That the Library grants access† to the public free of charge and to this end undertakes that if a Licence is granted:
   (a) The applicant(s) will display in a prominent place outside the Library building and visible to the general public a notice stating that access to the Library is granted free of charge; and
   (b) The applicant(s) will use his (or their) best endeavours to procure the local public librarian to display in the local public library or libraries a notice relating to the public relating to the applicant's(s') Library, similar to that referred to in (a) above.

4. That if a Licence is granted, the applicant(s) will not seek nor knowingly accept any consideration in cash or in kind, in breach of the terms of the Licence, in respect of or in connection with the supply to the Library of net books.

5. That the applicant(s) understand(s) that discount may be allowed under the Licence only in return for prompt settlement of invoices, and that no discount may be allowed on net books on which the bookseller(s) receive a discount of less than sixteen and two-thirds per cent plus five per cent.

6. That the applicant(s) understand(s) that books purchased under the Licence must be purchased solely for the use of the Library and not for resale.

This application is made on behalf of the following library:
(Please give the full name and address)

The applicant(s) nominate for the said licence the following bookseller(s) whose willingness to supply has been ascertained:
(Please give full names and addresses and attach a further sheet if necessary)

Date ....   (Signature) ....

                                          (Status) ....

* Please complete and attach any further information about the library (e.g. its date of foundation, specializations, size of stock, etc.) which might assist the Committee charged to consider this application. A copy of your last Annual Report, for example, would be useful.

† For the purposes of the Library Licence the word "access" shall be understood to mean (1) that the ordinary books in the libraries of the institutions concerned shall not be restricted to the use of the students or members of such institutional libraries, but (2) that under proper safeguards, and throughout the usual hours of such libraries, they shall be available, without charge, for public use within the library building. Satisfactory references or recommendations shall, where required, be submitted by strangers (as in the case of the British Museum), and discretionary power shall be vested in each library authority to withhold special works from general use, and to refuse to issue books to undesirable persons; but the free use of books shall not be unreasonably withheld.

22

The Quantity Book Buying Scheme (Revised November 1954)

A Scheme designed to extend the Large-scale Purchase of Net Books by Industrial, Commercial and Philanthropic Enterprises

What it is

The Quantity Book Buying Scheme, which was introduced by the Publishers Association and the Booksellers Association in 1937, was simplified in 1951 to provide for a discount to be given to those who *as an exceptional matter* ordered 12 or more copies of a title or titles, of which the total value was not less than £25. The scheme has now been amended and extended to cover large single orders for net books of an aggregate value of £250 or more, regardless of the number of copies of any one title contained in the order.

Conditions of Licensing

Licences for the grant of discount in accordance with the scale set out on page 182 will be issued by the Publishers Association under the Quantity Book Buying Scheme on the following conditions:

(a) The books must be required for gift or presentation in connection with the purchaser's business, or for philanthropic or propaganda purposes. The provision of a library, whether recreational or educational, for use by the purchaser's own employees, free of charge, would qualify.

(b) The books are not to be offered for sale by the purchaser, nor is their use or distribution to be made subject by him to any charge or other consideration.

(c) The order will be delivered in one consignment and paid for in cash on receipt.

(d) No discount shall be allowable on books on which the bookseller himself does not receive from the publisher a discount of at least 25 per cent. The value of any such books shall be deducted from the total value of any order coming under this scheme before application is made for discount to be allowed.

(e) Licences issued by the Publishers Association under this scheme shall apply to one order only and shall not be valid for repeat orders (although application may be made for fresh licences in respect of repeat orders that qualify on their own account).

The scale of discount allowable shall be as follows:

(a) *For an order for assorted titles worth £250 or more:*

Value of Order	Discount
£250–£349	5%
£350–£449	6%
£450–£549	7%
£550–£649	8%
£650–£749	9%
£750–and over	10%

(b) *For an order for a large quantity of one title (minimum 12), to a total value of £25 or more:*
A flat 10 per cent discount.

QUANTITY BOOK BUYING SCHEME

The Publishers Association

Application for Licence for the Allowance of Discount

To be completed in duplicate and sent to:

The Secretary, The Publishers Association, 19 Bedford Square, London WC1B 3HJ

I/We (Name of Firm)...

of...

hereby apply for a licence to allow discount to:—

(Name of Customer)...

of...

in respect of an order for:—

(Complete (*a*) for orders for **assorted** titles.)   (*a*) New net books to the value of £....................

(Complete (*b*) for orders for a quantity of **one** title.)   (*b*) ......copies of ....(title)

published by...

at........................(price).

being fully satisfied that the books are required for purposes within the conditions set out overleaf, namely:—

....

....

.....................(give details of exact purpose for which books are required)

and that the purchaser understands and will comply with the said conditions.

Signed......................................

Date.............................. Position in Firm.................................

For official use only.

To.. (booksellers)

of...

You are hereby authorised to allow a discount of.................per cent to

....on the above order.

Signed......................................

Date.......................... Secretary, The Publishers Association.

23

The Book Agency Scheme

Why it exists

In the course of his trade, the bookseller is often confronted with an organization which is in a position actively to promote the sale of books, but which cannot in any sense of the word be regarded as undertaking the normal risks and responsibilities of the bookselling trade. These organizations, such as churches, clubs and schools may often find that their local bookshops or even book-buying facilities by post do not fully meet their needs as far as stock is concerned, or are inconvenient to use owing to distance or times of opening. These organizations may have the capacity to encourage book-buying and actually to attract a number of firm orders. Publishers individually are not likely to open accounts with them and give them trade terms, so that the bookseller here has the opportunity to channel supplies through his own shop. In such circumstances, the question of discount inevitably arises. With a regular demand and a diminished risk of bad stock, the bookseller may reasonably feel that such business warrants the giving of a small discount. With net books, however, it would be a breach of the Publishers' Standard Conditions of Sale if a discount were to be given, *unless there were some authorization from the Publishers Association.*

What it is

This authorization exists in the Book Agents' Licence.[1] It is

[1] See also page 187, 'Book Agent's Licence for Schools'.

issued, after an examination of the circumstances, by the Publishers Association to the particular organization, and the licence will include the names of the booksellers who are entitled to give the organization a discount on net books purchased for resale. *This point is important*; the licence is issued to an organization as an *agency* for resale and it is not intended for organizations such as libraries and schools where the books are purchased for use. The agent has to undertake to resell the books at not less than the net prices. The discount paid must not, in the conditions of the licence, exceed half of that received as trade terms from the publisher by the bookseller himself; in practice it is usual for a discount of 10 per cent to be given.

How it is Done

The organization which requires the licence should apply to the Publishers Association for an application form (see below). The application must include the name of the supplying bookseller or booksellers, and the applicant should, of course, first make sure that the bookseller would be willing to supply on the agency conditions. Once the licence has been granted it is a matter for arrangement between the agent and the bookseller as to how often orders are made, and whether books can be returned. The bookseller should bear in mind that such business is done at a reduced gross profit, and that the discount given away is intended to cover the agent's own expenses and risk, if any.

THE PUBLISHERS ASSOCIATION

19 Bedford Square, London WC1B 3HJ

APPLICATION FOR A BOOK AGENT'S LICENCE

A registration fee of fifty pence should
be enclosed with this application

Name of applicant...
(*If you have a business, organizational or institutional name please show it*)
Address of applicant...
....

1 The applicant nominates for the said licence the following bookseller(s) whose willingness to supply has been ascertained:
(*Please give full names and addresses*)

....

....

2 What type of books do you propose to sell?

....

3 How much stock of books do you propose to carry?

....

4 Describe the manner in which you propose to sell these books

....

....

....

5 How do you propose to display the books to intending customers?

....

....

6 What special connections have you, if any, to facilitate the sale of books?

....

....

....

.... (signature)

Date

Book Agents' Licences are granted in consideration of an undertaking by the Licensee:

(i) not to offer for sale or to sell any new net book or books at less than the full net published price, either directly or indirectly or by way of settlement discount;

(ii) not to ask for or to accept any allowance upon new net books except from the Bookseller named upon this Licence or upon any endorsement thereof.

THE PUBLISHERS ASSOCIATION

19 Bedford Square, London WC1B 3HJ

BOOK AGENT'S LICENCE FOR SCHOOLS

Name
(If you have a business name, please show it)

Address

having applied for recognition as a Book Agent, and having given the undertaking printed on the back of this Licence, is hereby authorised to purchase new books: for resale to the public at the full published price, from the following bookseller, viz.,

these books being for recreational reading, entirely for resale at full published prices to individual purchasers (i.e. not for class or scholastic or library use) and the said bookseller is hereby authorised to allow the said book agent an allowance not exceeding fifty per centum of the retail discount given to the bookseller by the publisher in respect of each new book supplied to the book agent, BUT ONLY during the period for which this Licence is valid, and so long as the Licensee observes the conditions of his undertaking.

It is a condition of the granting of this Licence that it may be revoked at any time by the Publishers Association upon reason being given and upon its giving written notice by the hand of its Secretary to the parties named herein. But unless revoked on account of any action which the Publishers Association or the Joint Advisory Committee consider to be a breach of its terms and/or conditions three months' notice shall be given to the Licensee.

For and on behalf of
the Publishers Association

....*Secretary*

Date of Issue

Undertaking

This Licence is granted in consideration of an undertaking by the Licensee:

    (i) not to offer for sale or to sell any new net book or books at less than the full net published price, either directly or indirectly or by way of settlement discount;

    (ii) not to ask for or to accept any allowance upon new net books except from the Bookseller named upon this Licence or upon any endorsement thereof.

I/WE accept the terms and conditions of this Licence and undertake that they shall be observed in all dealings under its authority.

Signature of Licensee ....
       (*in full*)
Business name (*if any*)...

Business address...

....

....

Date...............................

24

Established General Trade Practice Regarding Allowances on Net Books

General

1. Allowances, in cash or in kind, at the publisher's discretion, are given only in the home market. Allowances are not generally given in respect of non-net books, juveniles or paper-back books.

2. Reductions in price, revised editions, cheap editions and remainders are customarily announced by the publisher in the trade press (which provides a section headed 'Trade Notices' for the purpose), regardless of when the books in question may first have been published.

3. Allowances are commonly given only on copies which the bookseller can show that he bought within six months prior to the announcement in the trade press, unless the book in question has been published for less than two years, if fiction, and for less than three years, if non-fiction.

New (Including Revised) Editions

4. The publisher's announcement of a new edition usually includes the date by which copies of the current edition should be returned for credit.

5. The publisher almost invariably gives credit on copies returned by the specified date either by the issue of a credit note or by supplying copies of the new edition to the same invoice value as those credited, as the publisher chooses.

6. When a new edition is issued *without notice* having been

given, it is generally considered that the publisher has a moral obligation to exchange copies of the previous edition within twelve months after the issue of the new edition.

Cheap Editions

7. Notice of a forthcoming cheap edition is customarily given not less than two weeks before it is due for publication.

8. When a cheap edition is issued within two years of first publication, if fiction, or within three years, if non-fiction, then the publisher, as a matter of practice, gives allowances in respect of claims made within one month of his announcement.

9. When a publisher issues a cheap edition which is designed to sell concurrently with the previous edition he naturally considers the extent to which the new edition may limit the sales of the old and usually gives allowances in respect of not less than half the number of copies of the previous edition held by the bookseller. (As indicated earlier allowances are not customarily given when a paperback edition is issued under licence concurrently with the publisher's own edition.)

10. When a cheap edition is issued *without notice* having been given, booksellers are generally regarded as eligible for allowances within twelve months of the issue of the cheap edition, as in the case of revised editions.

Reductions in Price

11. Books reduced in price are customarily treated as cheap editions for the purpose of allowances (see paras. 7–10, above).

Remainders

12. When remaindering within two years of first publication, if fiction, or within three years, if non-fiction, the publisher traditionally announces his intention not less than two weeks before the proposed remainder date.

13. When remaindering outside the periods mentioned in

para. 12 above, the publisher usually gives notice not less than four weeks before the proposed remainder date and such notice is generally accepted as implying that the publisher *forthwith* no longer requires his net price to be observed.

14. When remaindering within the periods mentioned in para. 12, above, the publisher normally gives allowances in respect of claims made within one month of the announcement.

15. When a book is remaindered *without notice* having been given, booksellers are generally regarded as eligible for allowances whenever they discover that the book has been remaindered, regardless of the date of first publication, but it is commonly recognized that a publisher who omits to give the customary notice may do so subsequently and thereafter accept further claims only for a period of three months from such notice.

✝✝✝✝✝✝✝✝✝✝✝✝✝✝✝✝✝✝✝✝✝✝✝✝✝✝✝✝✝✝✝✝✝✝✝✝✝✝✝

25

ISBN (International Standard Book Numbers)

The ISBN is the certain method of precisely identifying a book since the number is unique for each title in all respects, including edition and binding. It usually appears on the reverse of the title page but it would be a blessing if it also appeared with the price on every book jacket.

The number consists of four groups of digits. The first digit is o in the United Kingdom, the second group, consisting of one or more digits, identifies the publisher, the third group identifies the book, and the last is a check digit.

With the increasing use of computers and the use of visual display units for feeding orders to the computer, together with future developments such as Standard Account Numbers and an Orders GIRO, numbers, as compared with names and titles, become increasingly important. All new publications should be allotted an ISBN, which will almost certainly be vital when any system of Public Lending Rights operates.

The administrative control of the scheme is exercised by the Standard Book Numbering Agency Limited. It allocates identifying numbers to publishers and ensures that they create ISBNs in full to titles published by organizations or persons who do not produce their own, and registers and records all ISBNs.

Full details can be obtained from the Standard Book Numbering Agency Limited, 13 Bedford Square, London WC1B 3JE.

✦✦✦✦✦✦✦✦✦✦✦✦✦✦✦✦✦✦✦✦✦✦✦✦✦✦✦✦✦✦✦✦✦✦✦✦

26

BOD (Booksellers Order Distribution)

This service was designed to save booksellers both time and money.

Briefly the bookseller puts all his orders to various publishers *in one envelope* which he posts first-class mail to: Booksellers Order Distribution, 4 Grosvenor Road, Aldershot, Hampshire. BOD forwards them immediately by first-class mail *on the day of receipt* to the publishers concerned. There is no need for the bookseller to give publishers' addresses as BOD works from a most comprehensive index.

This service was born as a result of the frustration felt by certain booksellers who considered that a service run by booksellers to ensure speed and accuracy would be beneficial to the trade.

The charge is 2p per item (orders stapled together for one address count as one item). Accounts are rendered monthly; payment may be made through the Booksellers Clearing House. *Remember:*

BOD dispatches your orders on the day of receipt.

BOD always uses first-class mail.

BOD saves considerable time and money.

BOD is the only non-profit making order distribution service working in the interests of booksellers.

BOD offer research into obscure publishers' addresses at no extra cost.

BOD dispatches to selected Continental addresses.

27

VAT (Value Added Tax)

There is no tax on books. They are zero-rated. All the following are zero-rated:

Books, Booklets, Brochures, Pamphlets and Leaflets, Newspapers, Journals and Periodicals, Children's Picture Books and Painting Books, Music, Maps, Charts and Typographical Plans.

Many are confused into thinking that books are exempt. In fact, literally they are exempted from tax but books are not classified as *exempt*.

With zero-rating the article comes within the VAT system. It is, in fact, liable for tax but since the rate of tax is zero, the amount of tax to be paid over on the sale to the consumer is nil. However—and this is significant—as it comes within the scope of VAT the final seller, i.e. the retailer, may rebate back the tax which has already been paid.

Let us take a practical example. There will be special relief for books, newspapers and periodicals, etc. (as above). Up to the point of its final sale by the bookseller, a book passes through many hands. The raw material is paper; to the paper is added print; then there is the artwork; the blocks; the binding and so on; and each stage in its turn attracts VAT. If a book were given exemption it would mean that the bookseller would have to sell it at the fixed or recommended price, which would include all the VAT which had been added in the course of production. On the other hand, as the book is zero-rated, then the VAT in course of production is rebated.

This example should explain the difference between zero-rating and exemption and make it clear that, in general terms, zero-rating is to be preferred.

Booksellers should carefully record all VAT they pay and claim it back. In mixed businesses carrying, say, fountain-pens, stationery, etc. which are not zero-rated, extra care is necessary to obtain accurate dissection.

It is important to know that VAT is chargeable on postage and packing if shown separately on the invoice.

28

The National Book League

The National Book League exists to encourage the full use and enjoyment of books. Its many services are designed to inform and enlighten readers, both at home and abroad, to encourage suitable provision of books by public authorities of all kinds, and to heighten the possibility that books will be used widely and selected wisely.

Those who join may themselves benefit from the League's facilities and services. But also, because the League is a public society supported by the subscriptions of its members and recognized as an educational charity, they contribute to nation-wide and world-wide improvements in the use of the printed word.

Its address is: 7 Albemarle Street, London W1X 4BB.

The Scottish office of the National Book League exists to promote the League's aims in Scotland and to cater adequately for its Scottish members. Lectures and public exhibitions of current books are arranged whenever possible, and members in relevant areas are notified. News and articles of Scottish interest appear regularly in *Books*; this is the official journal of the National Book League. National Book League publications can be obtained direct from the Scottish office, which also maintains a wide variety of touring exhibitions for use exclusively within Scotland; and through the office members can make use of all other services of the League. Its address is: 1121 Paisley Road West, Glasgow SW2.

The National Book League is able to undertake a number of activities which no publisher, bookseller or library has the time or money to do alone, and in many ways it is of practical help to the trade as a whole. Its Book Information Bureau is one such service. The Bureau has a trained staff and the facilities to answer immediately many telephone inquiries about books which might otherwise take hours to track down, even assuming one had the necessary references. But the Information Bureau has more extensive references than a bookshop could afford. The Bureau can often give you quickly the publisher and date of publication; it can tell you whether an American novel has been published in England, and give information about forthcoming books. More difficult requests need longer research and are dealt with by the Bureau within a few days, often with recourse to the British Museum. Daily the staff increases its available information as it compiles new reference lists.

Other services of the National Book League are the Book Lists, which are compiled by experts and contain an annotated selection of books, with date of last edition and price. These are useful for booksellers and libraries as check-lists for stock, as well as for any individual wishing to make a special study of one particular field. Three or four of these have been published each year since 1949. In addition, the NBL publishes a number of specialized guides, such as F. Seymour Smith's *An English Library*, a list of classics and standard books, booklets on book collecting, the use of books and ways to select reading matter.

The National Book League with its various book exhibitions creates new links between the publisher, the bookseller and the libraries. The League has more than sixty exhibitions on tour at any time and these may be utilized by any member-library, bookseller, school or other organizations. Librarians and book-sellers and the public can thus examine new books at first hand and, if they want to buy, can order them for their own shelves. The general public particularly benefit by being able to handle and study books, and obviously often find books on interesting subjects to which they had previously given little thought, so developing new interests and enthusiasms; this encourages them to make more frequent visits to local bookshops and libraries.

The NBL exhibitions of current books are of two sorts:

general exhibitions including books on various subjects, such as 'New Books for Children', and books in a particular field, such as a domestic subjects exhibit. For example, a conference of teachers of domestic subjects may ask the League to assemble a display of books. This is done and after the conference the display is sent on tour elsewhere.

Perhaps a word should be said about the selection of books. In some instances, there are only a small number of new books in a given field, so that there is no problem, since all books can be included. In other cases—such as 'Fiction since 1945'—there is an attempt to combine variety with quality.

Committees of qualified men—usually either booksellers or librarians or critics, or all three—select the books. There will always be room for argument in any group over the choice of books, which must be limited. Sometimes, in fact, the interest of an exhibition is enhanced by the controversial nature of the selectors' decision. But by and large it may be said that the NBL aims to show the public not only a representative selection of books in each field but particularly the best books in each field.

The League's historical or scholarly exhibitions, which show books on a given subject over a period of centuries, or illustrate the literature of a region, have less direct effect on bookshop sales although, of course, the antiquarian bookseller appreciates them, benefits by them, and participates in their organization, even if only by lending rare volumes. But these, too, can be connected to modern books, for example through modern editions or critical works or biographies, and can do a great deal to stimulate interest in books.

The League is constantly working on new means to link bookshops with its activities, so that they may co-ordinate window displays and have in stock books which are likely to be in demand. Information about any exhibits may always be had by writing to the Director.

A special word should also be said about two other types of book display. The first is the Children's Book Week. The League is ready to help any library, school or other organization by supplying exhibitions of children's books (which can be supplemented by library stocks); also with lists of speakers with special appeal to child audiences. As many as a thousand children may visit a library in a week to see books, hear and see the speakers or take part in special quizzes and discussions. The NBL annotated book lists are useful guides to Children's books.

Of particular interest to the book trade are the British Book Design exhibitions held annually at Albemarle Street. By drawing attention to outstanding examples of book design, they foster a public desire for more readable and attractive books and give some insight into the means to achieve them; although most other NBL exhibits achieve the same results.

The other side of the League's function, that of educating the public to read more and to make a more selective use of books, is also carried on through the activities mentioned above. Exhibitions can reach people who have little or no contact with books, many of whom would never think of entering a bookshop. What happened, for instance, when in 1951 the League arranged to send an exhibition of five hundred books to schools? The evidence shows that children became interested in books that they might not have seen in the course of their school work, and that orders were placed on the demand of boys and girls who had seen the display. The same thing happens when men are shown new books that relate to their hobbies and crafts, or when books are put before Women's Institutes or social gatherings.

Finally. the use of the League's Georgian house (7 Albemarle Street, London W1X 4BB) as a club for all its members must be mentioned. The bar, snack-bar and public rooms make it a convenient place for members to meet. In the library there is a display of new books, changed monthly, which is a 'living review' and a service much appreciated by members. Thousands of members and their guests visit the house every year. In addition, the exhibitions in the gallery are an attraction to the visitor.

The library contains one of the best collections of books about books in the country, and books may be borrowed by members.

Summing up, it should be stressed that the League is a non-profit-making and non-partisan organization, and its members pay subscriptions to support its activities. There are also corporate members which include, for instance, schools and voluntary organizations. The membership is drawn from every quarter of the British Isles and, indeed, represents every continent. The League is still a new organization, operating without precedent; it has done much to promote the cause of books and to fill a serious gap in the book field. It is still experimenting and seeking new ways to carry on its work. It is always open to suggestions, since only by its liveliness and the vigilance of its members can it most effectively pursue its mission on behalf of books.

The NBL has fought many campaigns on behalf of books, and among its successes have been the exemption of books from tax and the improvement in school-library allocations. It has also campaigned ceaselessly but unsuccessfully against increases in the postage rates on books.

The National Book League's Summary of its Activities

The NBL, which is half of the AEC/NBL Working Party that triennially sets out recommended levels of school book grants and library levels, is responsible for huge increases in public expenditure on books.

The NBL produces book lists on everything from BASIC READING SCHEMES to MONEY MANAGEMENT. Some of these lists sell in their thousands. Most of them relate to an actual exhibition. ALL OF THEM INCREASE BOOK SALES by appreciable amounts.

The NBL answers 60,000 queries a year in its Book Information Bureau. Many of these lead to extra demand for books.

The NBL has over three hundred exhibitions annually touring the country, encouraging people to buy books. These range from FLOWER ARRANGEMENT to BOOKS FOR SMALLER COMPANIES.

The NBL promotes poetry evenings in the Queen Elizabeth Hall, in St John's Smith Square and in its own building. All of these lead to extra poetry book sales.

The NBL sponsored the Bedford Square Book Bang which reaped three home and four foreign television programmes, over thirty broadcasts, hundreds of inches of magazine and newspaper coverage, and £13,000 worth of EXTRA books sold.

The NBL administers the John Llewellyn Rhys Memorial Prize and takes part in the running of the Booker Prize.

The NBL mounts exhibitions for foreign books which are often exchange exhibitions for British books being shown abroad.

The NBL's Children's Reference Library is the only place in the UK where teachers can easily find one copy of every children's book published in the preceding twelve months.

The NBL's main library is among the best libraries of books on books in the country and its constant use by other library systems indicates its widespread propaganda value.

The NBL's display of BOOKS OF THE MONTH, a selection from the latest books published, is a constant shop window for its 6,000 members; and the countless other people who visit 7 Albemarle Street.

The NBL publishes a quarterly magazine, BOOKS, entirely devoted to publicising the enormous variety of books available.

The NBL is an impartial national spokesman for books when anything concerning them crops up at political and social levels.

29

Book Centre

Booksellers' supplies come either direct from the publisher or wholesaler or from Book Centre. Book Centre in brief is a kind of warehouse for a large group of publishers but it is much more.

Book Centre was founded on a co-operative basis in 1938 on the initiative of Sir Isaac Pitman & Sons Ltd. The object was to secure the economics and efficiency of large-scale operation not easily available to individual publishers. Book Centre today, with over 500,000 sq. ft of warehouses, transport depots and offices, offers comprehensive centralized and economic distribution and accounting services to publishers. It is the trade distributor and accounting service for over a hundred publishers dealing with well over 20,000 booksellers all over the world. On average it fulfils more than 20,000 orders a week from its warehouse stocks of over ten million volumes of more than 50,000 titles. In addition, it operates a computer bureau service which produces over 70,000 invoices every week.

Because of the size of its operations Book Centre provides a distributing and accounting service which is more comprehensive and efficient than most individual publishers can afford, and herein lies the main value of Book Centre service.

An additional advantage and saving to a member publisher is that much of his own office and warehouse accommodation can be surrendered, and clerical and warehouse staff released, leaving his executives more time to devote to the creative work of publishing. Publishers distributing through Book Centre do not have to bear any of the cost of distribution until sales have been realized and cash in respect of them have been received. Moreover, the cost is directly related to fluctuations in business—a matter of great advantage in the event of seasonal or other falls in business volume.

Side by side with warehousing and distribution goes detailed recording and accounting, with statistical analyses of great variety available from a third-generation computer complex.

Book Centre was developed with one objective in mind—to enable publishers to dispense with the detailed and expensive task of distributing their own books and the complicated statistical and financial accounting it entails.

Today Book Centre provides an ever-increasing range of services to meet the book trade's growing and complex demands. Whatever an individual publisher's requirements, Book Centre can provide him with the service, allowing no wastage of effort and maximum profitability on what might well otherwise be an unprofitable situation. These services range from Members' Full Service—a 'binder to bookseller' operation, from arrival of the books at Book Centre ex bindery up to collection of the money due, credit control, and payment to publishers—to individual ancillary services, such as a Computer Bureau Service, Book Deliveries, Packaging and Dispatch, all of which are available on an *ad hoc* basis to all in the book trade, whether members of Book Centre or not.

Members' Full Service

This is where Book Centre assumes responsibility from the moment the books arrive in the warehouse until the cash in respect of sales is collected and paid to the publisher, and includes:

Warehousing of forward stock sufficient to maintain the service required by the publishers' customers.

Receipt and editing of order and their execution and invoicing on publishers' terms.

Providing answers in respect of unavailable titles and recording dues and subscription orders for future dispatch.

Sorting, packing, dispatch and documentation—normally within two days after receipt of day-to-day orders.

Co-ordination of delivery to home and export customers.

Dispatch of review, inspection and free copies, as instructed by the publisher.

Maintenance of stock records, including daily minimum level and out-of-stock report advice to the publisher when his reordering 'minimum stock level' is reached.

Receipt of 'returns'.

Supply of daily stock movement tabulation to publishers.

Maintenance of sales ledgers, collection and remission of cash twice weekly.

Providing statistical tabulations and analyses as laid out under 'Computer Service'.

Warehousing and Delivery Service

This service is made available to all in the book trade with Book Centre's responsibility restricted to warehousing, which may include collection, packaging and dispatch or delivery against invoices, as and when required.

Ancillary and Bookseller Services

Publishers' Parcels Delivery Service

PPDS operates a parcel delivery service network specifically for the book trade covering the United Kingdom and Irish Republic.

The central sorting depot is based at Neasden, which acts as a receiving point for parcels from publishers who either deliver into the depot or whose parcels are collected by PPDS vans and brought to the central depot. In addition, some parcels are trunked direct to regional depots. Parcels are sorted then trunked to regional depots which are responsible for delivering direct to the customer. The depots are:

'Neasden	Serves London and an area to the north of London with a boundary the perimeter of which runs roughly on a line—Reading, Oxford, Cambridge, Chelmsford.
Kingswood	South-east England to the east of Southampton.
Frome	South Wales and South-west England.
Atherstone	Midlands and East Anglia.
Doncaster	Yorkshire, Derbyshire, Nottinghamshire, Tees, Tyne.
Southport	Lancashire, Cheshire, Northern Ireland and the Republic of Ireland.
Edinburgh	Scotland and Carlisle in conjunction with Menzies.

Packaging and Dispatch

This service is available on request and covers packaging and dispatch from Book Centre. It is suitable for publishers, booksellers, book exporters and mail-order houses and comprises a very useful emergency service, charged according to the work involved.

Bulk Storage

Bulk storage warehousing facilities are available at Book Centre Depots in London, Home Counties and Northern England. Rates are highly competitive and are available on application.

Overseas Booksellers Clearing House (OBCH)

With this service Book Centre provides free to overseas booksellers two stationery forms:

1. Instruction sheet addressed to OBCH Book Centre.
2. Remittance advice form.

In this way, Book Centre clears publishers' accounts from a single remittance sent by the overseas bookseller and to his instructions. This saves the overseas bookseller postage, labour and the high current bank charges. The charge made for this service is based on a clearing fee from the bookseller and the number of remittances from the publisher.

Computer Service

As part of its programme to be well in advance of the rapidly increasing throughput of business, Book Centre has kept constantly up to date in the application and development of computers.

It covers three generations of computers from the IBM 1401 and its introduction in the early sixties to the IBM 360/40 in 1966, and the introduction in 1970 of the IBM 360/50 with visual terminals for improved feed-in, faster and increased programming and more detailed data analysis. Operated through the Publishers' Computer Service, the IBM 360/50 provides a proven system to publishers and the facilities of a large computer complex at a cost which is substantially lower than the running costs of the individual systems.

The service provides data preparation facilities, invoicing, stock control, sales ledger, sales analysis, order recording, credit control and a very wide range of statistical information. Alternatively the Publishers Computer Service will undertake all the above services, leaving the publisher free to concentrate on warehousing.

IBIS Ltd also use the computer service to provide a sophisticated and highly selective mailing service to export markets covering trade outlets, library addresses, educationists, universities and technical colleges and secondary schools.

There are in excess of 350,000 addresses on file which can be selected in three basic ways: geographical area, class of address, subject interest or any combination of these three.

The versatility of such a computer network enables the publisher to operate his office with the minimum of experienced highly trained staff, with the facility for such detailed work to be carried out at Book Centre and more economically than he could provide for himself.

Looking to the needs of tomorrow, Book Centre's system development staff are constantly researching the uses of computers in publishing and distribution with a view to providing improved and additional services at lower relative costs.

Visual terminal units are in use to provide the latest editing techniques and real-time inquiry facilities.

✤✤✤

30

Orders Clearing

This service was started in 1955 and provides a central clearing office for booksellers' orders, not only at home but also abroad. The system is simplicity itself and the saving to booksellers is substantial. This is how the system works. The bookseller sends daily, or whenever convenient, all his orders for British publishers to IBIS Mailing Ltd, New Building, North Circular Road, Neasden, London NW10 0JG, enclosed in one envelope, marking the outside of the envelope with his name and the number of orders enclosed. Where he has more than one order for a publisher he pins them together and such orders are charged as one. Orders Clearing then sorts the orders into publisher pigeon-holes.

Orders Clearing, previously a department of Book Centre was taken over by IBIS Mailing Ltd in 1972. This company is owned by a number of book-trade interests and is run by a Board of Directors representing a wide range of experience, under the Chairmanship of Julian Blackwell and including the Managing Director of Book Centre.

The new Board gave it as their intention to expand Orders Clearing—already processing 8,000–10,000 orders every day—into a highly efficient organization processing quickly and cheaply the majority of book-trade orders. The Board also planned to introduce new services to rationalize the flow of information and publicity to bookshops.

Orders Clearing provides a very fast and reliable service. The service remains at its central location in the Book Centre building. Because of this location some 25 per cent of orders can be collected or delivered within a few hours of arrival; the majority of the remaining orders get guaranteed next-day delivery by van, and others go first-class post. This combination of delivery procedures makes Orders Clearing unbeatable for speed; its price is much lower than any alternative; and its sorting is efficient.

One major innovation has been to change the method of charging which involved a comprehensive book-keeping system to record items whose value was 1p each. To rationalize this a system of vouchers (see page 209) has been introduced. The vouchers can be enclosed with each batch of orders.

Orders Clearing Instructions

Orders Clearing provides booksellers with a fast and efficient system of sending their orders to publishers at a fraction of the cost of separate posting. The following notes will help users to get the best value from the services.

1. The charge is 1p for one or more orders clipped together for the same publisher. You can save money by pre-sorting by publisher.

2. Please DO NOT clip together orders for more than one publisher.

3. You need only the name for publishers listed in Whitaker's 'British Publishers and Their Addresses'.

4. For all other publishers you need the full address. We will research and forward any not fully addressed but reserve the right to make a retrospective supplementary charge of 3p for every order that involves individual research and forwarding.

5. Put all your orders together with the appropriate vouchers into an envelope, use the labels provided free by us, or address clearly to: ORDERS CLEARING, IBIS Mailing Ltd, New Building, North Circular Road, London NW10 0JG.

6. Vouchers of 5 orders each are, overall, the most sensible breakdown of units and we ask you to put in vouchers to the nearest value. For example, if you are sending 21 or 22 orders send 4 × 5p vouchers. If you are sending 23 or 24 orders send 5 × 5p vouchers.

7. Orders received without vouchers will be sorted and forwarded as normal but we will invoice 1p per order and 5p for each envelope

received. This additional 5p is to cover the extra cost of book-keeping and invoicing.

8. Please do not put orders for more than one publisher on one piece of paper.

Vouchers Order Form

TO   ORDERS CLEARING, IBIS Mailing Ltd,
    New Building, North Circular Road, London NW10 0JG

Books of vouchers available in the following values:

20 vouchers for 100 orders	£1.00
100 vouchers for 500 orders	£5.00
200 vouchers for 1,000 orders	£10.00
500 vouchers for 2,500 orders	£22.50

Please supply............books of vouchers containing.........vouchers

Cheque enclosed....................Please invoice us........................

Signed .... Company ....

Address ....

✼✼

31

Wages and the Wages Council

The Retail Bookselling and Stationery Trades Wages Council sit to decide the *Minimum* rates of pay, holidays and hours for employees.

Let me emphasize at the outset, because there exists confusion in the minds of employers and employees, the function of the Council is to recommend to the Secretary of State *the rates of pay BELOW which no one can be employed in the trade*. The Wages Council does not fix the actual wages, in fact very many booksellers pay wages in excess of the minimum rates.

With the exception of a few small shops in remote provincial towns, the wages actually paid to bookshop assistants are considerably higher than the Statutory Minimum required under the Wages Councils Act.

Under the Wages Councils Acts not only are the *minimum wages* to be paid to assistants in the retailing of books and stationery fixed but also the minimum holidays with pay.

All employers should obtain copies of the Orders,[1] as failure to comply with them renders an employer liable to prosecution. 'Notices issued by the Wages Council must be posted up and kept posted up in the premises where they can conveniently be seen by the workers. Penalty for non-compliance—a fine not exceeding £20.'

Booksellers frequently find the Wages Councils Act difficult to interpret, but the local Wages Inspector of the Department of Employment will be found helpful in giving guidance in case

[1] Obtainable from HM Stationery Office.

of difficulty. The rules on holiday with pay, for instance, are rather complicated by the fact that payments for holidays are due between 1 April and 31 October, *but employees qualify for such payments by service* up to 1 April. There are other clauses, however, regarding holidays, which employers must understand if they are to avoid costly error. Part-time assistants also come within the scope of these Orders.

Both Employers and Workers are represented on the Wages Council. The Booksellers Association is represented by a number of delegates, and other bodies such as the National Chamber of Trade, the Multiple Shops Federation and the Antiquarian Booksellers Association are also represented. There are also independent observers whose votes are important in the event of there arising any disagreement between the two sides (the Employers and the Workers).

Wages Councils are independent statutory wage-regulating bodies appointed by the Secretary of State for Employment. They consist of equal numbers of Employer and Worker representatives together with three independent members, one of whom is appointed Chairman.

Their powers which derive from the Wages Councils Act (1959) include the submission to the Secretary of State of proposals for fixing the statutory minimum remuneration of workers within their field of activity. Before submitting proposals to the Secretary of State, each Council is required to publish them and to consider representations about them.

The Secretary of State is required to give effect to a Council's proposals unless he decides to refer them back for reconsideration. The rates and conditions contained in the proposals do not have legal effect until an Order is made by the Secretary of State.

Enforcement is carried out by the Wages Inspectorate. The rates established by Wages Councils are minima only and without prejudice to the payment of higher rates. Statistics of average earnings now available from the Department of Employment's New Earnings Survey show that employees in Wages Councils industries generally receive more than the statutory minima.

The statutory minimum remuneration payable to assistants varies according to job classification, age and location. The wages tables are given under three areas: London area; Provincial 'A' area; Provincial 'B' area. (Definitions of these areas are included in the Order.)

Shop managers and manageresses come within the scope of the Order, as do all other workers including cleaners, messengers and porters.

'Application may be made to a Wages Council for a permit authorizing the employment at *less* than statutory minimum remuneration of any worker who, on account of infirmity or physical incapacity is unable to earn the statutory minimum.' Unless the incapacitated or infirm worker is the holder of a permit he is legally entitled to the full statutory minimum remuneration.

Booksellers employing adult workers with no experience can pay *below* the minimum the Wages Council tables for a period. There is a clause in the Orders dealing with these 'Late Entrants' as follows:

'The minimum remuneration during the first *six months'* employment of a worker (other than a shop manager, manageress, transport worker, cleaner, messenger, deliverer or porter) who enters or has entered retail bookselling and stationery trades for the first time at or over the age of *twenty years* shall be the appropriate remuneration specified in the Table reduced by the amount detailed in the latest Order.'

Overtime rates are laid down by the Order.

Government officials make checks all over the country to make sure employees are receiving their just dues and, though the Orders are a little difficult to understand, the local Wages Inspectorate will, as I have said, be only too ready to clarify any point.

It is always possible, of course, for anyone in the trade to inquire of the Director of the Booksellers Association and of representatives of the Booksellers Association on the Wages Council, as they also can often advise on regulations appertaining to wages.

I have served on the Booksellers Wages Council since it was first formed over a quarter of a century ago, and for some years held the office of Chairman.[1] In consequence I have been present while negotiations have been in progress, and feel they have achieved much in so far as they give some protection to the workers and provide a yardstick for the employer, but they have become something of a handicap, largely because many people tend to regard the minimum wages in the Wages Council Order as being the wages actually paid. The rates are low and, as I have said, usually much lower than good assistants are in fact paid, but, if quoted as the wages that are likely to be paid (and what other rates can be quoted?), they must tend to discourage recruitment.

Why, then, are not the minimum rates more realistic? This is a difficult question, but part of the answer is that the representatives on wages councils represent the interests of the small traders as well as the larger ones. They know the smaller man cannot afford to keep his staff if wage rates are too high, so they tend to go cautiously.

It appears that the time is probably ripe for there to be some kind of amalgamation of wages councils to lay down minimum wages and holidays for all engaged in retailing, but the book trade would perhaps benefit more if it had its own wages council. Bookselling is a very special business, which is why there is no tax on books and why the net published prices have to be observed. Books are zero-rated for Value Added Tax, not so stationery. All this proves the special nature and importance of the trade and that the best interests of all engaged in bookselling are most likely to be served if a separate wages council for the bookselling trade was set up.

In my view, bookshop assistants' basic minimum rates would have been higher had they not had to be linked with stationers', and anything that detracts from the progress of bookselling is a serious matter. Our fine export trade in books, over one per cent of the total exports of this country, is linked with successful

[1] The only bookseller to hold this office during this long period.

marketing at home. Bookselling is too important a trade in itself to be linked with, and in some measure controlled by, a Wages Council where true booksellers are in a minority.

32

Training Courses

The possession of a Diploma in Bookselling should be the aim of every bookseller. It is obvious that in the years to come such a Diploma and other qualifications will be necessary requirements for employment in the better, if not in all, bookshops. It is therefore important, and it will become increasingly so, for every bookseller and for every assistant in a bookshop to be properly qualified.

Under the Government's Industrial Training Act of 1964 a number of training boards were set up to encourage training at all levels of commerce and industry. The Distributive Industry Training Board was established in 1968, being the largest of the boards, and responsible for 400,000 different firms, which includes all booksellers. The aims of the board are:

1. To ensure an adequate supply of properly trained staff at all levels in the distributive industry.
2. To secure an improvement in the quality and efficiency of industrial training.
3. To share the cost of training more easily among firms.

Fortunately booksellers have been in advance, or at least up to date, as regards the training of assistants, and for many years courses have been arranged, with subsequent examinations and finally the Diploma awards.

The aim of the Booksellers Association's training is to produce efficient and self-reliant staff at all levels, in every type and size of bookshop. This in turn should produce more profitable bookselling.

The Training Committee plans courses in bookselling to implement this aim and to meet the needs of members and the standards set by the Charter Group.

Details of training and courses leading to the Diploma appear below. Full details of the syllabus and examination regulations are contained in a booklet called *Training for Bookselling*. For this and other training inquiries write to: The Training Officer, the Booksellers Association, 154 Buckingham Palace Road, London SW1W 9TZ; telephone 01–730 8214.

Diploma in Bookselling

The possession of the Diploma in Bookselling will entitle the possessors to call themselves 'Booksellers'.

Candidates who are Arts Graduates in English Literature of an approved British or Commonwealth University may apply to be granted exemption from taking Final Paper 3—Specialist paper or Modern Writing.

Candidates must have had three years' experience in a bookshop in membership with the Booksellers Association or themselves be individual Members.

Overseas candidates must have had at least five years' experience of bookselling in a bookshop dealing in books printed in the English language.

Candidates obtaining eight certificates with Distinction will have the words 'With Honours' added to their Diploma.

Syllabus for the Diploma in Bookselling

1   PART ONE
Paper 1: The Work Book* (a 3–6 month basic course)
Paper 2: Bookshop Practice (6 months)
Paper 3: Bookshop Bibliography (6 months)

     PART TWO
Paper 4: Bibliography & Classification (6–9 months)
Paper 5: Books & The Mind of Man* (1 year)
Paper 6: Bookshop Economics (6–9 months)

* There are no examinations for papers marked *; the student's work is assessed by the Tutor and awarded pass, pass with distinction, or fail.

PART THREE
Paper   7: Bookshop Administration (6 months)
Paper   8: An outline of Publishing and Book production (6 months)
Paper   9: Elective paper in a specialist subject,*
      or, Modern Writing (1 year)
Paper 10: Oral

The times against each paper are approximations, the actual length of time taken depends on the method of study.

2   EXAMINATIONS
Examinations lasting $2\frac{1}{2}$ hours are set for each paper and are normally held *twice* a year, on the second Tuesday in January and on the first Tuesday in June at various centres in Britain and the Irish Republic.

3   THE SCOPE OF THE SYLLABUS
For a shop with a small bookselling business the Work Book will probably be sufficient for training purposes; one with a larger number of books will need to complete to the end of Part One of the Diploma. Assistants who want to make bookselling their career will also complete Parts Two and Three of the Diploma Syllabus and will study by means of one-day schools, training courses, the correspondence course or other training courses provided by the Booksellers Association.

PART ONE

1   The Work Book
Candidates will be expected to complete a Work Book, which covers their day-to-day work in the bookshop, including the rudiments of book classification; customers' orders; display; elementary stock control; trade reference books; the structure of the Book Trade and the practical and theoretical aspects of salesmanship. The candidate is expected to write concisely about what he has learnt.

2   Bookshop Practice
Candidates will be expected to have a deeper understanding of salesmanship and customer relations; how stock is ordered and what is done with it when received. The display of stock, communication, the history of the Book Trade with reference to the significance of the Net Book Agreement, are also important.

3   Bibliography
Candidates will be expected to have a practical knowledge of the use of, and information available from, the standard trade reference books, and will be expected to show a knowledge of the standard reference books (dictionaries, atlases, etc.) that they sell in the bookshop. In addition, knowledge of the Bible, its versions and editions, and of the classics of English literature is necessary.

PART TWO

4 Bibliography and Classification

Candidates will be expected to understand the function of bibliography, and should be able to evaluate books for different purposes. Practical classification and arrangement of stock, with particular reference to paperbacks is needed, plus a knowledge of the key works in English and American literature, and art books, and general science and technology. Key works in History, Archaeology and biography; philosophy and religion; travel; Fine Arts other than painting; domestic arts; sports and hobbies, should also be studied.

5 Books and the Mind of Man

Candidates will be expected to complete a study book which has been planned on programmed lines. Candidates will be expected to give concrete, factual answers to the programmed questions, having done the necessary research in the set book. Some questions are 'open-ended' to give the student an opportunity to express his own opinions in a short essay.

6 Bookshop Economics

Candidates will be expected to understand the economic structure of the book trade; should be able to understand trade statistics; should be able to define gross and net profit; should understand the relation of gross profit to turnover; rates of stock turn; depreciation; stocktaking; principles of stock control and the value of the Book Token scheme to the bookseller.

PART THREE

7 Bookshop Administration

Candidates will be expected to have a knowledge of staff structure; systems of contracting to libraries, schools, institutions, and industry; mail order business; buying for stock; appreciation of a Profit and Loss Account.

8 Final Paper Two: Publishing in Outline and Book Production

Candidates will be expected to have a knowledge of the function and methods of working of:

A publisher's editorial department;
sales department;
distribution department;
publicity department;
Book Centre.

They should understand the parts of a book; book production, including types of paper, type faces, hand and machine composition, printing, reproduction processes, processes of illustration, costing, book design and binding methods and decoration.

9 Final Paper Three: Specialist Subject

Candidates have the option of taking Modern Writing *or* a choice of *one* of the following specialised aspects of bookselling, e.g.

Religious Bookselling

Technical Bookselling
University Bookselling
Foreign Bookselling
Children's Bookselling.

10 An Oral Examination will form an integral part of the Final of the Diploma course. A panel of examiners will sit at regular intervals and students may present themselves for examination at any convenient time during their final year, irrespective of whether they have completed their written papers for the Final Qualification.

Examinations are held twice a year in all papers on the second Tuesday in January and the first Tuesday in June. Candidates may sit for any two examinations, but not more than two on any one examination date. Past examination paper and application forms are available from the training officer.

How to Study

Local Schools of Bookselling

Classes covering Bookshop Practice, Bookshop Bibliography and Bibliography and Classification are organized by the local Branch Training Officers. They are usually day-release or evening classes run over a period of months and held during the early months of the year.

Residential Courses

The Training Officer organizes both trade-based courses and management courses. They usually last a week and are held at various centres throughout the United Kingdom between January and July each year. Subjects covered include:

Diploma Course	*Management*
Bookshop Practice	Training the Trainer
Bookshop Bibliography	Supervision
Bibliography and Classification	Middle Management
Administration and Economics	Senior Management

Details giving the dates, venue and programme of courses are published in the trade press and circulated to all members of the Association.

Correspondence Courses

All papers of the Diploma, except the three work books,[1] can be studied through Wolsey Hall Correspondence College, Oxford. Details of the courses, including reading lists and the costs are available from: The Director of Studies, Wolsey Hall, Oxford OX2 6PR. Students wishing to enrol for any of these Diploma subjects should write direct to Wolsey Hall.

Certificate in Distributive Management Principles

The ambitious student, who wishes to manage book departments in the large departmental and multiple stores, or who may wish to work towards general management or run his own business, can not only study the courses arranged by the Booksellers Association but can take one of the courses arranged throughout the United Kingdom at various Colleges and Technical Schools leading to the Certificate in Distributive Management Principles.

Examined by City and Guilds of London Institute, this is a two-year part-time or block-release course intended for managers and potential managers and designed to appeal to the whole field of distribution.

Candidates must be 18 years of age and hold one of the following qualifications:

The Diploma in Bookselling or
Two passes at GCE 'A' level or SCE 'H' Grade or ONC or OND or Scottish equivalent.

---

[1] Work Books: Paper 1 The Work Book (basic); Paper 8 An Outline of Publishing and Book Production; Paper 9 Specialist subject: University Bookselling. These are all available only from the Training Officer. The student's work is assessed by the tutor, who will award a pass or fail. There is no examination.

Subjects

Part A (1st year)	Part B (2nd year)
Management Distribution (Marketing Merchandizing I and Fundamentals of Distributive Management II)	Management in Distribution
	English or Scottish Law
Personnel Management	
Management Accounting	
Economics	

In addition to the subjects listed above, candidates will be required to complete a project for which at least 80 hours should be allowed.

This course is one of a great many 'Courses in Distribution' which are available. Students wanting further information including course location should write to: Library Information Services Division, Distributive Industry Training Board, MacLaren House, Talbot Road, Stretford, Manchester M32 0FP; telephone 061–872 2494.

The Distributive Trades Education and Training Council, 56 Russell Square, London WC1B 4HP has a course for a General Certificate in Distribution. It is designed to meet the needs of young people in the 15–18 age-group employed in the distributive trades.

Syllabuses and other particulars of the course and other courses open to all those employed in distribution, are obtainable from:

City and Guilds of London Institute, 76 Portland Place, London W1N 4AA.

East Midland Educational Union, Robins Wood House, Robins Wood Road, Aspley, Nottingham NG8 3NH.

Northern Counties Technical Examination Council, 5 Grosvenor Villas, Grosvenor Road, Newcastle-upon-Tyne NE2 2RU.

Union of Educational Institutions, Norfolk House, Smallbrook, Queensway, Birmingham B5 4NB.

Union of Lancashire and Cheshire Institutes, 36 Granby Row, Manchester M1 6DW.

Yorkshire Council for Further Education, Bowling Green Terrace, Leeds LS11 9SX.

33

The Book Trade Charity

There is one book-trade charity: The Book Trade Benevolent Society. Previous to 1962 there were two book-trade charities, The National Book Trade Provident Society and The Booksellers Provident Institution. For the past seventy years two independent book-trade friendly societies existed for the welfare of members of the trade in distressed circumstances. The Booksellers Provident Institution was founded in 1837, primarily to serve the London area; later, in 1902, The National Book Trade Provident Society was created, with a strong provincial interest. Both organizations throughout their history did excellent work and relieved much hardship, but the desirability of merging them into one single trade charity was long recognized, and they were finally amalgamated. The Society is therefore now the sole book-trade friendly society and charity, and upon it rests the sole responsibility both for relieving hardship and for securing from the trade that financial support which is indispensable for its work.

The trade charities were amalgamated officially and became the Book Trade Benevolent Society in 1970. This is registered as a benevolent society under the Friendly Societies Act 1896.

The society's great achievement over the years has been in the provision of accommodation in the Booksellers' Retreat at Abbotts Langley, Hertfordshire. Beautiful bungalows, centrally-heated, and other homes situated in spacious and charming grounds are provided for aged and needy retired booksellers and publishers or their widows. To this is added the granting of financial assistance to others who have accommodation but insufficient income to live comfortably.

This is achieved through the generosity of publishing and bookselling firms and individuals in the trade who make regular donations or who have donated bungalows. The charity has plans for building more homes and must constantly seek more and more support, not only to provide further homes but to maintain people in them.

The overhead costs of making good dilapidations, providing heat and light, etc., constantly increase and the demands on the charity grow as more people are cared for. Anyone in the trade can visit, by arrangement with the secretary, The Retreat at Abbots Langley, and anyone who is in need or knows of someone in need who may be eligible for benefit under the rules of the society should communicate with the Secretary, Book Trade Benevolent Society, The Booksellers Association, 154 Buckingham Palace Road, London SW1W 9TZ.

The Society has a President, a number of Vice-Presidents, Trustees, an Honorary Treasurer and a Board of Directors. The committees include The Retreat Committee, the Relief Committee and the Development Committee.

The full objects of the society and the benefits are as follows:

Objects

The Society is established for the charitable purpose of the relief or maintenance in necessitous circumstances of persons who are or have been engaged and employed in the Book Trade in Great Britain or Northern Ireland for one year or more, and their husbands, wives, widows and widowers, children, fathers, mothers, brothers or sisters, nephews or nieces, or wards being orphans, provided that in considering applications for relief priority shall be given to former members of Section I of the National Book Trade Provident Institution and provided further that preference shall be given to persons who are over the age of fifty or in sickness or other infirmity whether bodily or mental.

No member of the Society shall be eligible for benefit, but former members of the Society shall be eligible.

The Society may purchase, construct, improve or manage or facilitate or encourage the construction or improvement of dwellings, for occupation by persons who are eligible for benefit under the foregoing sub-clause, subject to the provisions of Rules 10 and 11.

Subject as aforesaid, the Society may accept donations, gifts and legacies upon or subject to any trusts or conditions.

Membership

There shall be the following classes of members:

(a) *Individual Members*, who shall pay an annual subscription of not less than £1.05 or such other sum as may from time to time be determined by the Board.

(b) *Trade Members*, who shall be individuals, companies or firms carrying on business on their own account in the book trade or trades ancillary to it, and who shall pay an annual subscription of not less than £10.50 or other such sum as may from time to time be determined by the Board. No individual, company or firm who is eligible for trade membership shall be eligible for individual membership.

(c) *Life Members*, who shall on admission to membership pay one subscription of not less than £12.60 or such other sum as may from time to time be determined by the Board. Former life members and fully-paid-up members of the National Book Trade Provident Institution other than those in receipt of benefit at the date of transfer shall be life members of the Society without further subscription.

A form of application for membership shall be completed by an applicant and forwarded to the Secretary at the Registered Office of the Secretary. The Secretary shall bring all applications for membership before the Board at their next meeting, and the admission of applicants to membership shall be decided by vote at that meeting.

Every member shall be bound in all respects by the registered Rules of the Society.

Subscriptions of new members shall be due immediately upon

election and (except in the case of life members) subsequently in every year on the anniversary of the first day of the month following the member's election to membership.

The Board may remit subscriptions in appropriate cases.

No member whose subscription is in arrears shall be entitled to vote at meetings of the Society. A member whose subscription is more than three months in arrears may be removed from membership by resolution of the Board.

Benefits

The Board or any Committee of the Board appointed for the purpose shall consider the circumstances of any individual eligible under Rule 3, who shall have applied for assistance while in necessitous circumstances. The Board or Committee shall allocate among the applicants or among such of them as in their judgement they may determine upon, the funds at their disposal or any part of them in such amounts, manner and way as they deem to be most expedient year by year.

Every application for assistance shall be forwarded to the Secretary, who shall lay the same with all requisite documents before the Board or any such Committee as aforesaid at their next meeting.

Should the case appear to require immediate relief the Chairman of the Board or, if the Board shall have delegated its functions under Rule 7 to a Committee, the Chairman of such Committee shall be empowered to give assistance prior to the meeting of the Board or Committee as the case may be. Such emergency action shall be reported to the next available meeting of the Board or Committee for approval. If such approval shall not be forthcoming, such assistance shall be terminated forthwith, but any payments already made shall be deemed to have been properly made.

The Board shall have power to terminate assistance to any person who shall by improper conduct render himself in the opinion of the Board undeserving of continued assistance from the Society.

The Secretary shall keep a list of all persons who are eligible for and are seeking admission to The Retreat and any such person may at any time apply to the Secretary for inclusion in the list.

On any vacancy occurring at The Retreat the Board, or any Committee appointed for the purpose, shall, subject as mentioned below, consider how the vacancy is to be filled. Vacancies may be filled from persons not on the waiting list and (other things being equal) preference shall be given to members who were formerly members of Section I of the National Book Trade Provident Institution.

The Board may resolve that where any company or individual (hereinafter called 'The Donor') has provided a dwelling or the cost of a dwelling at The Retreat, the Donor shall have the right to nominate the first candidate (being a person eligible under these Rules) to reside at the dwelling in question. In the event of the Donor not wishing to make such a nomination the Board shall fill the vacancy in the ordinary way. All nominations by a Donor under this clause shall be in writing under the hand of the Donor and shall be sent to the Secretary at the Registered Office of the Society.

The Board may also resolve that admission to any particular dwelling shall be restricted to a particular class of person, and may in suitable cases resolve that admission to a dwelling shall be conditional on payment by the occupant of a contribution towards the cost to the Society of their occupancy.

All occupants of dwellings at The Retreat shall be licensees and not tenants of the Society, and shall before admission sign a declaration accordingly, agreeing to conform to the Rules and Regulations and Bye-laws made from time to time by the Board or any such Committee as aforesaid.

Appendix I

Unesco Book Coupon Scheme

Unesco Book Coupons may be regarded as international currency for the purchase of books and certain other printed matter. The coupons are of values $1, $3, $10, $30, $100 and $1,000, and 'blank coupons' which may be made out for amounts from 1 to 99 US cents. They may be bought by individuals, or institutions, in local currencies, and are particularly useful in countries with currency difficulties. The rate of exchange is at the official rate for the US dollar on the day of purchase. In some countries the distributing body for the coupons adds a surcharge to their price. This should never exceed 5 per cent.

The Unesco Coupons are widely accepted throughout the world in payment for books (also for some other printed matter, films and scientific material). On request Unesco will indicate suitable sources of supply. The address is:

UNESCO Coupon Office, Place de Fontenoy, Paris 7ᵉ, France.

Appendix II

Publishers' Answers

The Publishers Association recommends that the following code of answers be used by all publishers for titles which are non-available:

1 Not known
2 On order. To follow shortly
3 Binding (date)
4 Reprinting (date)
5 Not Yet Published
6 New Edition in Preparation
7 Reprint under consideration
8 Out of Print
9 On Order Abroad

As the above code is not yet generally used, the following is the recognized code of answers for titles which are not available:

OP	Out of print, title discontinued, i.e. as far as is known will not be reprinted.
TOP	Temporarily out of print, no reprint at present in hand, i.e. will not be reprinted unless a new demand arises.
NK or NO	Not known, or not ours.
RP/6m	Reprinting, six months.
RP/ND	Reprinting, no date can be given.
RP/Shortly	Reprinting, available shortly.
RP/UC	Reprinting under consideration.
B/ND or Bdg/ND	Binding, no date can be given.
B/6w	Binding, may be ready in six weeks.
B/10 Aug.	Binding, will be ready 10 August.
NP/ND	Not published, no date can be given. This is sometimes shown as NYO—not yet out, or NP and NYP—not yet published.
NE/6m	New edition in preparation, may be ready in about six months.
OO/USA	Out of stock, but on order from USA.
OTO/USA	Only to order from (e.g.) USA.
QP	Query publisher.
TF	To follow.
NE/ND	New edition in preparation, no date can be given.

Appendix III

Book Clubs

Book Club Associates, Strand House, Portugal Street, London WC2H 8DT. Tel. 01-240 1054.
    Kings and Queens of England
    Literary Guild
    Mystery Guild
    World Books

British Printing Corporation, 49–50 Poland Street, London W1H 9AB. Tel. 01-437 0686.
    History Book Club
    Military Book Club

Churchill Press Ltd, 2 Cecil Court, London Road, Enfield, Middlesex. Tel. 01-366 4551.
    Constitutional Book Club

David & Charles Ltd, South Devon House, Railway Station, Newton Abbott, Devon. See Readers' Union Ltd.

Folio Society Ltd, The, 7 Albemarle Street, London W1X 4BB. Tel. 01-730 9001-5.

Foyle, W. & G. Ltd, 121 Charing Cross Road, WC2H 0EB. Tel. 01-437 5660. TA, Folibra, London WC2H 0EB. Telex 261107.
    The Book Club
    Catholic Book Club
    Children's Book Club
    Garden Book Club
    Quality Book Club
    Romance Book Club
    Scientific Book Club
    Thriller Book Club
    Travel Book Club
    Western Book Club

Heron Books, 18 St Ann's Crescent, London SW18. Tel. 01-874 0441.
    Collector's Editions Club (simultaneous publication)
    Mystery Book Guild
    Valentine Romance Club

History Book Club Ltd, St Giles House, Poland Street, London W1. Tel. 01-437 0686.

Merlin Press Ltd, 12 Fitzroy Square, London W1P 6JD.
  Merlin Book Club

Odhams Mail Order Books (a division of the Hamlyn Publishing Group Ltd), Astronaut House, Hounslow Road, Feltham, Middlesex.
  Companion Book Club
  Herald Sun Readers' Book Club (Australia)

Peter Peregrinus Ltd, PO Box 8, Southgate House, Stevenage, Herts.
  Books for Professionals. The Professional Library

Readers' Union Ltd, South Devon House, Newton Abbot, Devon. Tel. Newton Abbot (0626) 3251. TA, Books, Nabbot. Telex 42904.
  Country Book Club Ltd
  Gardeners' Book Club
  Readers' Union Ltd
  Science Fiction Book Club
  Sportsman's Book Club
  Victorian (and Modern History)

SCM Press Ltd., 56 Bloomsbury Street, London WC1B 3QX. Tel. 01-636 3841. TA, Torchpres, London WC1B 3QX.
  The SCM Religious Book Club

Town Bookshop, Enfield, Middlesex.
  Booklovers' Guild

Weller's (Paul) Direct Book Service Ltd, Blackjack Street, Cirencester, Glos. GL7 2BZ.
  Collectors' Book Club

Appendix IV

Book Sizes

		Size in inches (uncut)	mm (approx.)
F'cap 8vo	Foolscap octavo	$6\frac{3}{4} \times 4\frac{1}{4}$	170×110
Paperbacks usually trimmed to		$7\frac{1}{8} \times 4\frac{3}{4}$	180×120
Cr. 8vo	Crown octavo	$7\frac{1}{2} \times 5$	190×125
Lge cr. 8vo	Large crown octavo	$8 \times 5\frac{1}{4}$	205×135
Sm. demy 8vo	Small demy octavo	$8\frac{1}{2} \times 5\frac{5}{8}$	215×145
Dmy 8vo	Demy octavo	$8\frac{3}{4} \times 5\frac{5}{8}$	220×145
Med. 8vo	Medium octavo	$9 \times 5\frac{3}{4}$	230×145
Sm. roy. 8vo	Small royal octavo	$9\frac{1}{4} \times 6\frac{1}{2}$	235×165
Roy. 8vo	Royal octavo	$10 \times 6\frac{1}{4}$	255×160

Appendix V

Glossary of Trade Terms and Abbreviations

Addenda (plural of *addendum*): additional material supplied in a book usually to correct mistakes or to bring matter up to date.

Ad hoc: special, arranged for a special purpose.

Appendix: (plural appendixes) supplementary material to the text of a book.

BA: The Booksellers Association of Great Britain and Ireland.

Belles-lettres: writings of a literary kind.

Blurb: the publishers' sales-description of a book, usually printed on the jackets and mostly eulogistic.

BOD: Booksellers Order Distribution (see page 193).

Book club: members agree to purchase books selected or issued for a period. Terms vary.

Bookplate: not to be confused with 'plates' which are separate pages of illustrations in a book. A bookplate is usually one sheet of paper, pasted inside the front cover, carrying a coat-of-arms, the name of the owner, or identifying the book with a special library or collection.

Bowdlerize: to take from the original text objectionable words or morally objectionable elements. Thomas Bowdler, from whose name the word is derived, issued in 1818 an edition of Shakespeare omitting words and expressions 'which cannot with propriety be read aloud in a family'.

BPRA: Book Publishers' Representatives Association.

Circa: literally means 'about'. It is used by antiquarian booksellers in their catalogues when an exact date is unknown but an approximate one can be given, such as *circa* 1756.

Clo: cloth binding, understood where no specification is made.

Colophon: an inscription or device identifying the publishing house.

Edition: the whole printing issued at one time from the same type (see Impression). A first edition is a book from the first printing. A book from a second printing is a second impression.

Ed.: Editor, edited by.

Endpapers: blank leaves, sometimes of coloured or decorative paper, at front and end of book.

Erratum (plural *errata*): error in printing.

Ex-libris: this means literally 'from the books' (collection of). These words usually appear at the top or foot of a bookplate.
Ex-library: a second-hand book sold from a circulating library or other library.
Expurgate: to take out objectionable matter from the text (see *Bowdlerize*).

First edition: (see *Edition*).
Fol.: Folio size.
Format: the shape, size and form of a book.

Impression: a printing or reprinting of a book from standing type or plates without alteration. If changes are made in the text the book is then a new or revised edition.
Imprint: the name and address of the publisher or printer, usually on the title-page, or at the end of the book.
ISBN: International Standard Book Number.

Jacket: (see *Wrapper*).
Journey terms: best terms, higher than usual, given on orders received by a publisher's representative, on his personal visits.

Limited edition: usually means a numbered limited edition. That is a special printing of which a limited number only is made, each bearing a number. The type is destroyed when the printing is finished.

NBL: National Book League.

Omnibus volume: a thick volume containing several books formerly issued separately, or a miscellany.
On Sale or Return: unsold stock may be returned for credit after a specified period.

PA: The Publishers Association.
PLR: Public Lending Rights.
PPDS: Publishers and Booksellers Parcels Delivery Service (page 204).

Recto: the front of the leaf and the right-hand page of a book.
Remainders: publishers' surplus stock sold on the understanding that it can be offered to the public at less than the original published price.
Royalties: an author's payment from a publisher on copies sold.

See safe: copies unsold, usually after an agreed period, may be returned for stock. Note the difference between 'see safe' and 'on sale or return' (see pages 31–2).

Signature: a letter or number by which the correct order of printed sheets is indicated to the binder.

Travellers' orders: orders received by publishers' representatives on their personal visits (see *Journey terms*).

Verso: The left-hand page of a book, which is naturally the back of the leaf.

Wrapper: dust-jacket or jacket—the paper wrapper round the covers of a book.

Appendix VI

Abbreviations used in Book Catalogues

A.L.S.	contains a signed autograph letter
bdg.	binding
bds.	boards
ch.	charts
col.	coloured
cr. 8vo	crown octavo
d.	diagrams
d.w. or d/w	with dust wrapper
edit.	edited
edn.	edition
facs.	facsimile
figs.	figures
fol.	folio
fr.	frontispiece
ill. or illust.	illustrated, illustrations
imp. 8vo	imperial octavo
l. or lthr.	leather
l.e.	limited edition
l.s.e.	limited signed edition
M.	maps
mint	condition as new
MS.	manuscript
N.D.	no date; this book is not dated
P.	portrait
pl.	plates
pp.	pages
r., r.e.	revised, revised edition
roy. 8vo	royal octavo
roy. 4to	royal quarto
S.	series
16mo	sexto-decimo
sm. 4to	small quarto
tabs.	tables
t.e.g.	top edge gilt
Tr.	translation

12mo	duodecimo
v.	very
v.g.	very good condition
vol.	volume
wrs.	wrappers

Appendix VII

Some Important Addresses

	Telephone nos.
Antiquarian Booksellers' Association 154 Buckingham Palace Road, London SW1W 9TZ	01-730 9273
Book Auction Records Dawsons of Pall Mall, Cannon House, Folkestone, Kent	0303 57421
Book Centre Ltd PO Box 30, North Circular Road, Neasden, London NW10 0JE	01-459 1222
Book Development Council, The (Export Division of the Publishers Association) 19 Bedford Square, London WC1B 3HJ	01-580 6321-5
Book Market, The The Clique Ltd, 109 Wembley Park Drive, Wembley, Middlesex HA9 8HG (Books for sale, medium for the antiquarian trade)	01-903 0494
Book Tokens Ltd. 152 Buckingham Palace Road, London SW1W 9TZ	01-730 9258
Books and Bookmen Hansom Books, Artillery Mansions, 75 Victoria Street, London SW1H 0H2	01-799 4452
Bookseller, The J. Whitaker & Son Ltd, 13 Bedford Square, London WC1B 3JE	01-636 4748
Booksellers Association of Great Britain and Ireland, The 152 Buckingham Palace Road, London SW1W 9TZ	01-730 8214-6
Bookwise Service Ltd Catteshall Lane, Godalming, Surrey	04868 5384-6

British Council, The
Books and Publications Section, 59 New Oxford
Street, London WC1A 1BP   01-499 8011

British National Bibliography Ltd
7 and 9 Rathbone Street, London W1P 2AI   01-580 3681

British Stationery and Office Equipment Association
6 Wimpole Street, London W1M 8AS   01-580 9256/7 3121/2

Clique, The
The Clique Ltd, 109 Wembley Park Drive,
Wembley, Middlesex HA9 8HG   01-903 0494

Hodgson's Rooms (Sotheby & Co.)
115 Chancery Lane, London WC2A 1PX
(Auctioneers of Libraries and Rare Books)   01-405 7238

International Book Information Service
New Building, North Circular Road, London
NW10 0JG   01-459 7221

Library Association, The
Ridgmount Street, London WC1E 7AE   01-636 7543

London Library, The
14 St James's Square, London SW1Y 4LG   01-930 7705

National Book League, The
7 Albemarle Street, London W1X 4BB   01-494 9001
(Book Information Bureau)   01-494 3501
Scottish Branch, 1121 Paisley Road West, Glasgow
SW2, Scotland

Publishers Association of Great Britain and Ireland,
The
19 Bedford Square, London WC1B 3HJ   01-580 6321-5

Society of Authors, The
84 Drayton Gardens, London SW10   01-373 6642 0900

Society of Bookmen, The
(Hon. Sec. David Whitaker)
13 Bedford Square, London WC1B 3JE   01-636 4748

Sotheby & Co.
34/35 New Bond Street, London W1A 2AA
(Auctioneers of books, works of art, etc.)   01-493 8080

Standard Book Numbering Agency
  13 Bedford Square, London WC1B 3JE   01-636 4748

Wages Councils (Office of) Retail and Bookselling
  Trades Wages Council (Great Britain), 12 St.
James's Square, London SW1Y 4LL   01-930 6200

Watt, A. P. & Sons
  26–28 Bedford Row, London WC1R 4HL
(Literary Agents)   01-405 1057

Appendix VIII

Starting a New Bookshop

The first questions asked by people new to the book trade are:

1. How do I obtain supplies at Trade Terms?
2. Is it necessary to become a member of the Booksellers Association to obtain Trade Terms?
3. How do I get Book Tokens?

The short answers are as follows:

1. An application must be made to the Publishers Association for your name to be added to The Directory of Booksellers. Once application is accepted you are in The Trade. There is a Registration Fee. The details required are given on the form below which is reproduced from the original document.
2. No, it is not necessary in order to obtain Trade Terms, but it is necessary to obtain Book Tokens.
3. Application must be made to Book Tokens Ltd, but see (2) above.

Application for Name in the Directory of Booksellers

(This is the form to be completed by those wishing to obtain trade terms)

THE PUBLISHERS ASSOCIATION

*All communications
to be addressed to
The Secretary*

19 BEDFORD SQUARE,

LONDON WC1B 3HJ

To THE SECRETARY,
THE PUBLISHERS ASSOCIATION

Date.....................................

Sir,

I/WE hereby make application for the addition of my/our name to the Directory of Booksellers maintained by the Publishers Association.

I/WE have completed the questionnaire overleaf, and enclose a registration fee of Five Pounds, which fee is to be returned in the event of the Council being unable to grant this application. It is understood that neither the grant of this application nor the acceptance of this registration fee will confer membership of the Publishers Association or of any other Association.

Signed..

On behalf of..

(*Contd. on page 242*)

1. Name...
       (*State whether Mr., Mrs. Miss, etc.*)

   Title of Firm...

   Business Address ....

       ....

2. State exactly as possible the area you
   propose to serve.   ....

3. Description of business premises:

   (*a*) Is it a Shop, Office, Stall or
        Private House?   ...   .

   (*b*) (*i*) Will it be, or is it, open to
        the public, and if so, at
        what times?   ...   .
        (ii) If not, to whom will it be,
        or is it, open? ...   .

   (*c*) (*i*) Is it on the ground floor?
        (*ii*) If not, where is it?   ...   (*i*).................. (*ii*) ....

   (*d*) Has it a frontage and en-
        trance on a thoroughfare?   ....

   (*e*) Is there a shop window for
        the display of books? If so,
        give dimensions   ...   .

   (*f*) (*i*) For how long have you
        been in occupation of
        these premises? ...   .
        (ii) If not now in occupation,
        when will you be?   ...   .

4. What class of books will, or do, you
   deal in, e.g., new fiction, cheap
   fiction, children's books, educational and technical books reli-
   gious books, general literature?   ....

   (*a*) Will, or do you (*i*) carry a
        stock of books, or (*ii*) obtain
        them to order?   ...   ...   (*i*).................. (*ii*) ....

(*b*) How much capital do you propose to invest, or have you invested, in the purchase of (*i*) new books (*ii*) second-hand books? ... ...   (*i*) £................ (*ii*) £............

(*c*) Do you, or do you propose to, stock books:
(*i*) for resale? ... ...
(*ii*) for purposes of a circulating library? ... ...

(*d*) (*i*) Do you, or do you propose to, carry a stock of books for sale all the year round? ... ...
(*ii*) If not, during which season? ... ...

5. Do you, or do you propose to, carry on any other business than bookselling at the premises described in the answer to No. 3? If so, give *full* particulars ...   .

6. What steps do you, or will you, take to further the sale of books?   ....

7. What is the total shop area available for the sale and display of books? ... ...

8. If your business in books is new, how will it provide
(*a*) An improved service to the public? ... ...   (*a*) ....
(*b*) A service at present not available? ... ...   (*b*) ....

9. What length of experience and of what type have you had in the book trade? ... ...

Any other relevant information or observations may be detailed overleaf.

Signature..............................

Please give address to which communications should be sent if other than as above.

....

....

Date..............................

....

....

This questionnaire when completed to be returned to:

THE PUBLISHERS ASSOCIATION
19 BEDFORD SQUARE,
LONDON WC1B 3HJ.

For Office Use Only.
RECD. ....
FORM D ....
FORM I ....
RESULT: FORM ....
N.B.A. ....

Index